Marriage by Divine Design

Marriage by Divine Design

Biblical Principles of a Winning Home Team

J. D. Towns

ISBN-13: 978-0-578-52372-9

Cover design by Luisito C. Pangilinan
All Illustrations by Tasha D. Towns

The Home Team
Louisville, Kentucky
United States

www.TheTeamAtHome.com

We live during a time in history where biblical principles for marriage and family are minimized or disregarded as old fashion or irrelevant. The result? Many Christian marriages are failing or barely maintaining. In *Marriage by Divine Design*, J.D. invites the Christian family to rediscover its biblical roots in order that they might thrive. In this book, the author gives the Christian family an appropriate word pointing them to the grace of God, which motivates and empowers them towards obedience and action.

—Dr. Jamaal Williams
Lead Pastor, Sojourn Church Midtown

There is no greater need in our society today, than to see the family thrive again. In this helpful and biblical book, J. D. Towns, answers questions and provide solutions for the common family. If you are a newly married couple or a couple that has struggled to work together as a team, read and heed the biblical principles included in this book.

—Angus Dickerson
Senior Pastor, Spillman Memorial Church

J.D. Towns offers a creative introduction to what the biblical family should look like. The genius of the book is that it fuses together biblical principles, practical examples and a portrait of the development of Abraham and Sarah. After reading *Marriage by Divine Design*, you should have an expectation of learning and enhanced hope for your marriage.

—Jared Lafitte
Founder and CEO, Mandy AI Inc

Marriage by Divine Design calls the family to rediscover its biblical roots. We are in time in history where family and marriages fail to lean on biblical principles. Couples across the country are struggling to faithfully follow the Lord in their marriage. This book is a godsend to call families to action and back to Christ.

—Steven A. Weber
Pastor, House of Faith Christian Church

J.D. Towns has wonderfully brought forth biblical principles to maintain a loving and long-lasting relationship between husband and wife. I recommend this book as a guide to assist couples planning to share a lifelong loving relationship. I also recommend that you exercise wisdom by practicing the principles provided.

—Al and Mrs. Marge Brown
Retired Pastor & Founder of Spirit Riders Ministry, Walnut Street
Baptist Church

About the Author

J. D. Towns, is a best-selling author and lead planter of Transformation Church in Christ. He is president of The Home Team, a ministry organization committed to the goal of equipping families through the word of God. He holds a business management degree from the University of Louisville and a Master of Divinity from the Southern Baptist Theological Seminary. J. D. is currently pursuing a doctorate degree at Southern Seminary as well. He and his wife, Tasha have one daughter, Natalie. He is a husband, father, pastor and servant of the Lord. He and his wife call Louisville, Kentucky home. Above all things, J. D. loves to spend time with his girls and the Lord through the Word. He and his wife have spent years exploring God's design for marriage. They strongly believe in the sufficiency of Scripture and the effectiveness of biblical counseling. They are excited to witness transformation in the lives of other families through the simple application of Scripture.

Dedication

Your life and your walk have truly been a blessing. You inspired and challenged us through your ministry as a wife.

You consistently spoke life to those you encountered. Your prayers and encouragement were of great value.

We loved you as a sister. We respected you as an elder. We appreciated you as a gift from the Lord. We beheld your personality as a dear friend. Even though you are with our Heavenly Father now, we will hold to your memory with great joy. We love you greatly and I just want to say…thank you!

Wife to Wardell, Mother to Nyckole, Matriarch & Special Member of the Towns Family.

Johnetta Towns Darden
Of Evanston, Illinois
1957-2019

—J. D. Towns

Table of Contents

List of Figures

Foreword

When I first met J.D. Towns, it was through my husband Keith. My husband shared with me that their longtime friendship began during his ministry leadership with youth and families. It turns out that during the time Keith was the Youth Minister and Director of the Family Life Center for a church in Louisville, Kentucky, as a teenager Jason attended various youth events. He would often attend church with his best friend, while in high school. My, husband, Keith, recalls that he displayed a focus and a determination that would be used by the Lord in His time and in His way. Initially unaware to my husband, Jason looked at him as a mentor while participating in the ministry events and that relationship has grown over the years. He has happily served as a staff member of Fellowship Christian Athletes (FCA), in which my husband has been involved in for quite some time. I also have volunteered with the ministry as an opportunity to share Christ with female athletes. He is a humble man who is serious about the word of God and sharing it with others.

This book is a great resource and tool for those contemplating marriage, engagement, newly married, and those couples who have many years of marriage under their belt. It can be used as a tool to "start a great fire" as well as to "keep the fire lit" in a marriage relationship. That fire represents Jesus Christ. A divine marriage must start with Him, and He must be kept in the midst of the relationship at all times, for the fire to stay divinely lit. The most important aspect of *Marriage by Divine Design* is that the foundation is biblically sound. The title is superb in of itself as it clearly represents the treasure you can expect to receive when you open the book for your reading pleasure. There is nothing like reading the work of an author and you get the sense that his or her work comes from a personal place of experience. It can help the reader to keep focus, with the anticipation of what's ahead. J.D. Towns has written a playbook that includes step by step divine strategies for the marriage relationship to strive for excellence. Please notice that I said "excellence" and not perfection. The term "excellence" refers to the intentional practice to do and live in such a way to glorify God. In the view of being a woman who happens to be a born-again believer, I am more in harmony with my relationship with God, who is the creator of femininity. God not only created the woman, but He provides clear instructions in His word about our role as women. It is imperative that we know and understand who God has called us to be as women. God ordained family and He divinely created what was needed to exemplify a godly union – a divine marriage between a man and a woman. My husband and I have been married 12 years, and on this journey together we have experienced some good and bad. During my review of this book, I can honestly admit that my husband and I will have it in a safe place to refer to for our own personal needs, as well as using it as a resource when ministering to couples. Although the title clearly states marriage, I would encourage single women who desire to be married as well as women who may have adapted to the feminist mindset, to read this book. There is a familiar saying, 'there is no "I" in team'. The Bible informs us that when a man and women come together in marriage, they are one flesh. From the biblical perspective, 'there is no "I" in one flesh". We are so very thankful for obedience to the Lord in writing this book. The author is not ashamed of the gospel and has a strong desire for other home teams to be victorious as well. We are thankful for our relationship with him, Tasha, and Natalie. This has been an awesome and humbling inspiration in more ways than one.

Marriage by Divine Design, uses relevant terminology through the prism of sports with a Biblical Worldview. The concept of 'Team' in a marriage is revolutionary in terms of what makes a team successful. Jason captures the essence of building the marriage, maintaining the marriage, thriving in marriage, and doing the things in a marriage that most people might not see or take it for granted. To have a winning 'Team' one must know their opponent, study their plays, and most importantly every couple must always keep 'watching game film'. With great anticipation my wife and I are looking forward to having *Marriage by Divine Design* in our possession. This book will equip, encourage, and elevate our marriage. It will be a useful study resource for coaching potential couples and edifying other married couples. When it comes to having a marriage that is headed by God the Father, centered by God the Son, and directed by God the Holy Spirit it will be a victorious 'TEAM' because Together Everyone Achieves More.

In His Grip and In His Word

—**Pastor Keith S. and Lady Tanisha R. Hackett**
Senior Pastor and First Lady
Greater Salem Baptist Church, Louisville Kentucky

Preface

A winning home team does not mean a perfect home team. No one has a perfect relationship. Even our relationship with God is flawed but only because we are flawed as humans. Things become a little messy when TWO humans get together and decide to become ONE. A winning home team still has passionate disagreements but can find a resolution. A winning home team overlooks faults and focuses on unity through love. A winning home team enjoys the time they spend together. A winning home team loves, serves and is ever seeking the Lord. Trials come upon winning home teams also, but their foundation sits on the solid rock of Jesus Christ.

There are families everywhere that have begun with great intentions and vivid visions of what the family will become. Some of these visions may have begun while daydreaming as a child. Some young ladies who played with Barbie dolls or watched Cinderella dream about eventually getting married to a knight in shining armor. Some men have dreams of having a great career and having a family that loves them even more; a family that they can lead. The American dream sometimes is explained as having a nice house in a suburban cul-de-sac, two and a half kids and a puppy. Including summer vacations with lots of fun and laughter.

Have you become surprised to realize that many of your expectations were not met? As families have created their vision, they have also devised their plans to reach that vision, but the Lord was very seldom consulted. The worldly plans promise so much but deliver very little. Christ offers something much better. Many need God to lead them instead of trying to lead themselves.

This is the purpose of Marriage by Divine Design. It is not meant to be an exhaustive book on marriage. Instead, it is meant to be a resource for families that finally want to put their plan in God's hands, giving God an opportunity to construct a winning home team. Marriage by Divine Design is meant to extract some of these pertinent principles and help you implement them within your home team. When the word of God is applied within your life, your family's change will surely come.

I pray that this book will be a blessing to your marriage as your home team looks to incorporate God's design and looks to experience the abundant life that God has for you.

"For I know the plans I have for you," declares the LORD, "plans to prosper you and not to harm you, plans to give you hope and a future" (Jeremiah 29:11).

May the Lord Bless Your Family,
The Towns' Home Team

Acknowledgements

I am extremely grateful for the following people who helped to lay a spiritual foundation in me that will always exist.

The Lord Jesus Christ, everything that I have and that I ever do is only because of your love, grace and mercy. Following you has been by far the greatest aspect of life. Thank you for saving me and making me brand new.

Darlene Towns – Mom, I am indebted for your sacrifice over the years. Thank you for instilling in me commitment and devotion to the Lord. Many years ago, I did not understand your words but I now understand your heart behind it. Thank you for your prayers and always staying by my side. Your encouragement has been powerful. None of this would have been possible without you being in my corner.

Mozziz DeWalt – Pops, I am grateful for our friendship. Thank you for encouraging me to think outside the box and challenging me to not settle. Our numerous talks over the years have been a true treasure.

Towns family – Joshua, Loretta and Mamie – Thank you for raising me as your son. I learned so much by watching and listening to you all. You sacrificed and invested so much into my life. Thank you for pointing me to Christ. I miss you all very much and your memory is strong in my heart. We shall meet again when the trumpet blows!

Jefferies – Donna & Earnest – I have been blessed by observing you all over the years. I may not have said much but I learned so much from you both. Dominique and Deonna, love ya much. Follow the Lord and pursue your purpose.

Jones – Beverly & Donald – thank you so much for your support over the years. Mia- your consistent encouragement and prayers have been refreshing. Montez- thank you for your help and advice. L.B., Landon, Starr and Tyre, keep the Lord first in all things ...it is the key to the abundant life.

DeWalt family – Nannis & Paw Paw I am so grateful for your love and wisdom. We miss our Bible studies in the kitchen. We learned much about the Lord and marriage from you. Aunt Charlotte – Tasha and I are extremely grateful for your counsel and your guidance as we prepared for marriage. Even with bad health, the image of you dancing at our wedding, was the sweetest thing. Thank you for spiritually investing into us. Without your prayerful support we may not have made it past engagement.

My Extended Family in Chicago – you may be miles away but your prayers are felt. We love you dearly. Our roots run deep and those roots are anchored in Christ Jesus. I am very proud and grateful for the witness of our late patriarch, William Henry Towns Jr.

Willie Wilcox – brother I have not and will not forget about you. You have always been and will always be my brother. Our childhood was so alive and so is your memory in my heart.

Brown family- Thank you for being an extended family. I will never forget the joy that Carlton and I had at your home. You always treated me as family. It was a blessing to witness a godly marriage and family through you.

Linda Cash and Jermaine – I will not forget the unlimited hours of joy that we shared. I smile every time I think about those memories. You will always be family.

Daniel family- Mrs. Veronica, thank you for being such a loving and godly woman. I am glad that God connected me with Lamar because I gained another mom. You always treated me as your own. Thank you for allowing the Lord to minister through you. I marveled at how you interacted with your husband so gracefully. I was also amazed by Mr. Daniel's peacefulness. Thank you so much.

Morris family – Mr. Ken & Teri I have been blessed to gain two parents. The Lord knows that I needed you both. I thank God for your union. We have enjoyed the good days and some tough days together. My life has been blessed through you. "the Gang" also demonstrated a biblical version of what true family is. Thank you for loving me regardless of my faults. I am forever grateful. You will always hold a special place in my heart.

Terrence & Xiomelkis Morris – Sister thank you for your contribution to this work. Boy is my brother blessed to have a great wife and mother in you! Terrence- I don't know how my life would be without our brotherhood. We have laughed together, got in trouble together and now have been transformed by the Gospel together. Wow, what a journey! I am so proud of your professional accomplishments and talk about you all of the time. I am most proud of the husband and daddy that you have become. God is making a generational impact in your home team! I am thankful to God for ordaining our brotherhood. Man, this has been a wild adventure! The Lord has surely been gracious.

The saints at Spillman Memorial Church – Thank you for your consistent love. You have been involved in every spiritual phase of my life. I received my spiritual foundation through you. Thank you so much for being a blessing from day one. Your encouragement and prayers have been empowering.

To the saints at Transformation Church in Christ, thank you for your labor of love through prayer. I have truly needed your support.

The Towns Home Team - Wow! Tasha, God could not have granted me a better friend and teammate to walk with. I just love our talks over coffee. Thank you for listening to my jokes that I "thought" were funny. Thank you for being my friend and a great mother. I am proud of the woman that you have become. Natalie – the day that you were born is the day that I shall never forget. You are such a blessing to your mother and I! We thank God for you all the time. Remember to follow Jesus because He loves you even more than we do.

THE HOME TEAM

INTRODUCTION

One of my favorite pastimes is doing puzzles with my 6-year-old daughter. She enjoys it just a little more than I do. She is at the age where she needs my help. However, she is also at the age where she feels like she can do everything by herself. Natalie really wants to prove that she's big enough. Sometimes my job is just to encourage her and champion her success. I sometimes just let her "figure it out". However, without assistance, she may never complete the puzzle. She is oozing with optimism, but puzzling is not a strong area in her life yet. My responsibility is to coach her to completion when she allows me to do so.

It is possible that you have apprehended this book and you are experiencing marital bliss. Maybe you excel at communication and conflict resolution in your marriage. Perhaps your marriage is full of harmony. Even when there is a disagreement you handle it with great grace and maturity. If this is you, I hope and pray that you learn principles that you can apply in making your marriage even stronger.

However, you might be like much of society. Maybe you strongly desire to experience great joy and fulfillment in your marriage. You started with great expectations and hope of what the future would bring. However, things have not turned out the way you would have liked and you have struggle to get the family train back on the tracks. Does this sound like you? Just like Natalie, it has been an absolute struggle to get pieces to fit and fulfill the family puzzle. If this is you, please understand that there are many people that are in the same boat. My hope and prayer is that some of the principles mentioned in the following pages will both challenge you and encourage you as you pursue what God has for you.

Puzzling is very similar when it comes to marriage. Couples across the country are trying to fit puzzle pieces where they need to go. The missing piece of the puzzle is God's model, the Gospel. It transforms perspectives and completes the family puzzle. There are some puzzle pieces that just do not fit. These puzzle pieces include Romanticism, hyperfeminism and hypermasculinity.

The World's Design

As the culture has become increasingly secular, marriages have struggled even more. In the real world, what happens in relationships never occurs by accident. There are only two designs that are available. The Devil has offered his design which is packaged as the world. It is very shiny on the outside but rotten in the core. The adversary has come to steal, kill and destroy everything relating to God and the institute of marriage. Within the world, the focus is self-satisfaction. Kostenberger asserts the same, "It can be rightly said that marriage and the family are institutions under siege in our world today and that with marriage and the family, our very civilization is in crisis." (Kostenberger 15). As a result, families need to be prepared for the opposition and schemes that they will face.

Cultural changes have been used as an attack on the family over the years. Many families are ruled by worldly ideologies and have suffered as a result. Only homes that are founded on the solid rock of Jesus Christ will be able to stand against the ever-changing cultural norms. Dr. Willie Richardson (2016) explains it well:

"We are constantly reminded by television talk shows and social and behavioral scientists of the overwhelming number of dysfunctional families. Compared to pre-1972, there is the statistical fact of high divorce rates year after year."

What is evident in our world today is a clashing of cultures. Unfortunately, division is usually the result.

This is the reality for many families and has become the norm. This does not have to be so. These attacks have come in many forms over the years. Modern ideologies have been presented as solutions, but the family unit has gotten weaker. Here are a few:

Masculinity

Hyper-masculinity is a psychological term used to describe stereotypical male characteristics that are extreme in nature. These characteristics include but are not limited to extreme aggression, a high value of physical strength, control and an unhealthy perspective towards sex and women. These types of mannerisms have been perpetuated through some media and entertainment. There are movies, television shows and even video games that present these things as entertainment. Many young boys grow up with a distorted perspective of what real masculinity is.

Hyper-masculine attitudes tend to come across as insensitive and inconsiderate. This mindset is often counterproductive and antagonizes unity and harmony within the home. Wives who are married to such a person feel voiceless, undervalued and unloved. It is hard to communicate when you feel like you are not being heard. Unfortunately, men with this attitude struggle to see what is taking place. Wives receive it as a lack of love and an unloving environment is not conducive for a God-glorifying marriage.

This becomes an issue when men seek to enter a harmonious relationship through marriage. Ultimately, hyper-masculinity can possibly err on the side of alienating the rest of the family and focusing on pursuing selfish desires. Over time division is the result and men often feel misunderstood. It is a model that is presented by the world and adopted by many of its inhabitants. However, it is not a model that is identified in Scripture. I will seek to elaborate on God's model of masculinity in chapter 1.

Feminism

Feminism was founded with the fundamental goal of achieving equal rights for women. This was a necessity due to the great inequality and suffrage at the hands of a male-dominant society. Equality was not offered, and women had to fight for it. Women did pursue justice and the culture and some modern societies are more sensitive to many of these issues. Equality has been achieved in many areas and much is owed to the historical trailblazers that initiated the movement.

One of the best aspects of feminism is helping the culture to understand that women have the same value and worth as men. This is nothing new. This truth has been revealed from God, in the Bible, since the very beginning.

Over the years, feminism has morphed into many different forms. For some the idea of feminism has created much confusion. Some modern elements of feminism have opposed the traditional and biblical ideal of marriage. However, some radical elements produce an unhealthy attitude towards men. Some women pursue independence and strength in their femininity. None of the above are godly perspectives that can be supported by Scripture. These radical aspects would fall under hyper-feminism.

Some people see marriage as an outdated patriarchal system that is extremely oppressive to women. Modern feminism preaches equality, but some women seek female dominance as a result. Some women may think that life is better without a man because they do not need a man. This mindset will present the marital union as a curse when God intended for it to be a blessing.

Some modern aspects of feminism also encourage independence. Some women try to express their strength by saying that they do not need to depend on men. Independent mindsets have often created friction in romantic relationships. Some try to prove their ability to succeed without the help of a male counterpart. Educated and talented women have taken on the responsibility of leading the home because they had no other choice. These women responded out of necessity to hold their family together. God has created spouses to lean on each other and live in community. However, for the Christian, there is no such thing as independence. The Christian walk is designed for husband and wife to always depend on God for everything and to live by His grace.

However, these things become evil when they are idols in our hearts. Even rights, if pursued more than a relationship with the Lord, become great stumbling blocks. True marital fulfillment, joy, and peace are only found in following God's design.

Feminism is all about the pursuit of equality. Feminism is not inherently bad in of itself. The Bible has always declared women to be equal with men and commanded that women be treated with love. Listen to what the Apostle Peter said; "likewise, husbands, live with your wives in an understanding way, showing honor to the woman as the weaker vessel, since they are heirs with you of the grace of life, so that your prayers may not be hindered." (1 Peter 3:7 ESV). The human-made system has many flaws. Some men can be oppressive and domineering, but this is not endorsed by the Lord. Some women fear that they will obtain a husband that will lord over them with dominance. God is so conscious of the treatment of wives that He will be slow to answer the prayers of an unloving husband. Do not be confused, God will righteously deal with the oppression of women.

Hyper-Feminism, just like hypermasculinity, promotes selfishness and seeks to achieve utopia and comfort at all cost. The worldly model seeks to fix the problems of society. However, God's model seeks to starts on the inside to change the hearts of individuals.

Whether male or female, we are at our best when we seek and consider the needs of others. We are at our best when we seek to put our will to the side and pursue God's will for our lives. I will elaborate on God's model of femininity in chapter 1.

Romanticism

Romanticism is an ideology that began in Europe in the 1750s. It was embraced as an artistic movement. Romanticism is about the expression of love. Since it has been thrust into society, our understanding of love will never be the same. There are some distinctives that are the result of Romanticism.

Romanticism is extremely hopeful about the idea of marriage. Marriage is promoted as a life-long love story that is full of pleasure. Marriage does involve love and should be pleasing. Marriage is a lifelong love story but not in the way that Romanticism has tried to recreate it. The ideology of romanticism has tried to present a life that is void of adversity. A problem-free life is just not realistic.

Romanticism has also attempted to merge love and sex. Sex as the ultimate expression of love is a myth of romanticism. For this reason, many confused individuals pursue sex before they even have a real understanding of what love is. This is backwards and subverts the marriage before it even gets started.

Romanticism has encouraged prospective spouses to follow their heart – emotions and feelings reign supreme. Decisions made are based on perceptions that are created by emotions. If your feelings turn sour, then the relationship has failed to please you. This is a dangerous way to think because emotions are fickle. Romanticism assumes that the heart is trustworthy enough to follow and is inherently good. The Bible declares, "The heart is deceitful above all things, and desperately wicked: who can know it?" (Jeremiah 17:9). Following the heart is unwise. The passions of an unregenerate heart will lead you away from God and into an unfulfilled life.

Romanticism also tends to focus on self-satisfaction. It is true that romance is and should be included in a loving marital relationship. Sex is and should be included in a loving marital relationship as well. However, neither sex or romance true expressions of love in of themselves. The world does not understand what true love is and that is why many marriages and relationships struggle. If relationships are built on romance, what shall we do when the romance fades? If marriages are built on the sexual satisfaction, on what shall we stand when our bodies fail? Sex and romanticism are temporary joys but love is everlasting. The world does not understand what real love is. The common thread in Scripture from cover to cover, is God's love. This will create the unbreakable bond and the thriving fire your marriage needs to be fruitful. We will take a closer look at true Godly love in chapter 6.

God's Design

God's design is the opposite of the world's design. The world's system is run by Satan. God has given us a Divine Design for marriage that leads to victory. God's design demands order and requires commitment. God is not the author of confusion. God does everything orderly.

God's will is that husbands and wives become spiritually mature. When a woman knows the lord well, she will thrive as a wife. When husbands love God enough to submit to His will, they will excel as the leader of their home. In order to embrace God's design, we have to be willing to put the worldly things behind us and embrace what God has for us. Today, God is calling for men and women to embrace their God given identity that is found in the Word. These two realities will always be at odds with each other. A choice will have to be made.

God had purpose, intent, and design when He created marriage. God intended both genders to live in harmony and not in isolation. The problem is not God's design for marriage. The real problem is adults within the system who have no real relationship with the God of heaven. When a true man of God operates in God's design for marriage, it is a true blessing to his wife and will bring her great joy. When godly women are led by the Lord in marriage, husbands are greatly encouraged.

My objective in the following pages is to expose you to ancient principles that prove to be true and effective. The origin of these principles is the Word of God, which is absolute truth and wisdom. I do not promote myself as an expert. God is the expert that I am promoting. Guidance needed to experience a blessed marriage is found in His Word, which is sufficient. However, people often struggle to apply biblical principles to their lives. My goal is to aid in that application. We will look at the profound and progressive relationship between Abraham and Sarah found in Genesis.

Each Chapter will contain team jewels. These are general principles of wisdom that will help you focus on application. Each chapter will contain questions at the end. The purpose of this is to provide a time of reflection and prayer for you and your spouse. It is a time to allow God to reveal what is hidden in your hearts. As true thoughts and emotions emerge, compare them to what has been commanded in God's word. If it fits with the Word, then continue in it. If it is contrary to the Word, get rid of it. Consider it an opportunity to do some spiritual housekeeping.

Team Jewels

1. Spend time communicating with your spouse to produce clear vision. Spend time in prayer to request God's grace, strength and guidance for His vision.
2. Leadership provides freedom and peace when your life is guided by the Lord.
3. If I win, my home team wins too. We will win together. We will rise and fall TOGETHER!
4. Make it a big deal to celebrate any blessing that God sends to your home team. Make it fun and encouraging. Find things to celebrate with gratitude.

5. Keep your relationship with the Lord as number one. The relationship with your spouse needs to be next. Allow nothing to disrupt those two.
6. Regular family devotions are refreshing for the home team.
7. Let God lead you to identify foundational principles that your home team will adopt.
8. Incorporate a weekly time of rest. Consistently set time aside to spend with your spouse. Be okay with saying no to anything that tries to interfere.
9. Analyze team expectations that exist between you and your spouse. Make them biblical and realistic.
10. Change is great when God is leading it. If He is, do not resist but embrace the newness.
11. Listening to your spouse is righteous. Be careful not to allow your emotions guide your decisions.
12. God will use your family experiences as a learning opportunity.
13. Forgiveness produces Freedom. Try it today.
14. God does not go back on His promises. You cannot control when or how He moves, but remember that God is faithful.
15. Your home team needs a unified vision. Synchronize with your spouse, synchronize with the Lord. Let Him provide the vision and submit to it.
16. Maintain your hope and joy in all situations. Both are contagious and are found with the Lord.
17. A family that sits and eats together stays together.
18. Worship God and nothing else. Idols of the heart need to be removed.
19. Make dinner time important in your home. Become invested in communicating with your family.
20. Trusting God for His provisions means trusting God for His protection.

CHAPTER **1**

TEAM CAPTAINS

"Too many kings can ruin an army."
–Homer

Although expressed within the context of an army, Homer's quote captures the essence of a team. Just like an army with soldiers and a team with players, a family has members. Without a designated leader, there will be no sense of direction. There will be no defined roles and responsibilities. Don't expect a victory. Don't expect a championship. Don't expect a marriage by divine design.

A thriving marriage by divine design requires a team captain to set the vision. A vision inspired by God that will serve as a guiding light for the home team to follow so that they can love more, laugh more, pray more and express gratitude more.

As such, it is important to designate a team captain, to maintain a vision, to avoid worldly influence and to fulfill one's role.

In some cases, a team captain may be leading the team without the team knowing it. The movie Karate Kid demonstrates this well. The leader had a clear sense of direction, but it came across as very unorthodox to the follower.

The Karate Kid generated excitement and empowerment among young people. The movie was able to connect with the personal feelings of teenagers. Many youths related to the awkward feeling of not-fitting-in in certain environments. Daniel Larusso was new to Los Angeles and recently moved there with his family. Daniel was a little scrawny kid that was clearly a mamma's boy. He was not the outgoing type but began to develop a friendship with Ali. Daniel may have gained a friend, but he quickly developed enemies as well.

Daniel finds interest in the wrong girl who was recently in a relationship with a karate master with much attitude. Johnny is still fond of Ali and takes offense to her interest in Daniel. Johnny is not alone but has a posse of guys that are equally unhappy with Daniel's existence. After several awkward moments at school with Johnny around, Daniel is convinced to attend a mixer after school. An argument occurs, punches are thrown, and Daniel is left with a bruised ego and a battered face.

No one stepped forward as a real advocate for Daniel. He expresses to his mother that he does not like his new school, but he has only been there for a few weeks. Running back to New Jersey was not an option either. His mother will not allow him to ditch school; he must return the next day to face his peers, more danger and embarrassment. Daniel is totally out of solutions.

Daniel came up with a master plan. It was sparked by a conversation with his unique neighbor, Mr. Miyagi. Daniel believed the answer to his prayers was learning how to defend himself and he had just found his sensei. The two seemed to be total opposites. Mr. Miyagi was much older; they both came from contrasting cultures. It seemed like they had absolutely nothing in common. Mr. Miyagi had a strong accent, and his way of doing things seemed very weird to Daniel. However, they had some things in common. The beauty of the movie is that they both needed each other. Mr. Miyagi was also a transplant in Los Angeles and was originally from Okinawa, Japan. They both needed a relationship. Daniel needed an experienced teacher, and Mr. Miyagi needed a willing pupil. A special bond was created. They would soon become great friends, but a huge challenge was ahead of them – teaching Daniel karate and self-defense.

Mr. Miyagi agreed to train Daniel and teach him the ways of karate. Daniel was ecstatic. He initially wanted to defend himself but soon built up the courage to compete in the local karate tournament. Daniel was full of excitement, but he had never actually witnessed Mr. Miyagi teach Karate.

Mr. Miyagi's karate workout was very unconventional. Daniel was brand new to karate, so he had no idea what to expect. Mr. Miyagi would have Daniel do mundane tasks like waxing his car and sanding his floor. He spent all day laboring at these tasks. When the destination began to get blurry, he aggressively showed his displeasure. Daniel became frustrated because he was expecting a more conventional approach. Daniel said that doing chores was not what he signed up for. He wanted to learn real karate!

Mr. Miyagi then showed him that he had been teaching him karate all along. Daniel was well on his way to becoming a karate master, and he did not even realize it. Daniel blindly follows his teacher's leadership even though he had no idea where it would take him. Mr. Miyagi did not inform him, in advance, of the methodology. He only promised to teach him karate. To learn self-defense and win the karate tournament, Daniel would have to put complete trust in Mr. Miyagi's leadership. To fully trust Mr. Miyagi, Daniel had to trust his methods. Likewise, to fully trust in God means to fully trust in God's methods for your life.

Team Captains

Every team needs a leader. Corporations have CEOs, countries have presidents, teams have coaches, and choirs have directors. In sports, the coach provides the ultimate guide for the team. However, coaches will often identify a teammate who is mature and respected enough to be a leader amongst their peers. Coaches expect to have the team captain work with other team members. Being a team captain requires maturity. A strong team captain has the ability to lead their team to higher heights.

In the same manner, your home team needs to have a designated leader. God should be the head coach of your home team. Each team member should continue to receive directives from the Lord. Furthermore, God has designated husbands to be the team captain and head of the home team. Listen to the words of the Apostle Paul.

> *"Wives, submit to your own husbands, as to the Lord. For the husband is the head of the wife even as Christ is the head of the church, his body, and is himself its Savior. Now as the church submits to Christ, so also wives should submit in everything to their husbands." (Ephesians 5:22-24).*

This scripture identifies God's design for the structure for the family. Within this structure, husbands are called to submit to the Lord as well. Both spouses are called to submission to the Lord. Knowing the Lord as Savior is wonderful, but He needs to become Lord over your life as well.

Biblical Manhood and Womanhood

The world culture is always trying to redefine things. The culture is never stable. However, the Bible has always been consistent. Let's establish a framework of what the Bible identifies a woman and a man to be. Biblical manhood and womanhood denotes spiritual maturity. There is no one size fits all and the specifics may look different based on how the Lord leads each family. There is no definition to give but the Bible gives various descriptions from Genesis to Revelation. Here are some qualities to consider:

Manhood

1. Leadership – Men ought to lead by serving. Mark 10:42-45
2. Protection – Men should be the first to make sacrifices in order to protect their family. Ephesians 5:25
3. Provision – Men should do their best to provide for their family by depending on the Lord as their primary source. 1 Timothy 5:8
4. Discipline – Paul encouraged Timothy, a young man, to live a life of self-discipline. 2 Timothy 1:7
5. Love – Men are not suggested to love their wives. It is a command! Ephesians 5:25

Womanhood

1. Beauty – Outward beauty fades but a woman of God always possesses inward beauty. 1 Peter 3:3-4
2. Submission – Wives are called to submit to their husbands as unto the Lord. Ephesians 5:22
3. Help – Wives are to be advocates and helpers for their family. Genesis 2:18
4. Respect – Wives are not suggested to respect their husbands but it is commanded. Ephesians 5:34
5. Nurturer – Wives are called to spiritually nurture other young women. Titus 2:4-5
6. Keepers of the home – Wives are called to tend to and be gatekeepers of the home. This is also spiritual in nature. Titus 2:5

Maintain Vision

Leadership has everything to do with vision. A leader is unable to lead without knowing where he is leading the followers. Jesus Christ is the greatest leader of all time. Since Jesus is divine, He is also all-knowing. His foresight is perfect and trustworthy. The Lord sees what you cannot. So, trusting in His foresight creates challenges and requires faith. John Maxwell explains the importance of vision.

If you lead your team, then you are responsible for identifying a worthy and compelling vision and articulating it to your team members. However, even if you are not the leader, identifying a compelling vision is still important. (Maxwell 92).

Having vision is extremely important for any team to succeed. Since our vision only reaches so far, it is wise to allow the Lord to guide your family. God will not force his vision upon us. Instead, we are called to embrace it willingly.

The Greatest Leader

Matthew, just like the other disciples, found it difficult to follow Jesus. They had never encountered someone like Him. He offered a simple request, follow me (Matthew 9:9). That seemed very simple on the surface, but it required leaving behind what he valued the most. Matthew was busy working but had to stop his plan in order to follow the plan that Jesus had for him. This is a pretty hefty request when you have absolutely no idea where you are being led.

Jesus did a great job of casting His vision of the Kingdom of God. He shared several characteristics of the Kingdom. Jesus told of angels (Luke 20:35-36). He talked about heavenly mansions (John 14:1-6). It was not uncommon for a large multitude to follow Jesus because of the power that He possessed. This was demonstrated by the wonderful miracles of healing and deliverance. His words and actions provided an expectation of what the Kingdom of God would represent.

After casting a vision of the Kingdom, Jesus requested that the listeners respond by embracing the Kingdom. All of this sounded great, but a response was mandatory. The initial hesitancy of the disciples proved they had not yet fully trusted their leader. Receiving the Kingdom required self-denial and humility (Matthew 18:3, Luke 9:23).

To the defense of the disciples, it is very difficult to wholeheartedly follow someone when you have no idea where they are going. You may not understand God's vision and design for your life. However, it is best for you to trust in the Lord as your leader by trusting in His design for your marriage. Let the Lord cast His vision for your family.

Team Jewel
What vision has God given your home team? Invest time praying and communicating with your spouse about the vision God has cast for your family. Ask for God's grace, strength and guidance to reach the vision He has provided.

Follow the Leader

Consistency

Consistency is critical. It is especially important to follow God when things become uncomfortable and awkward. Without consistency, it will be hard for others to trust your leadership. Following God requires determining that you will continue, even when things make no sense. Bumps on the journey tend to cause knee jerk reactions to revert to following the plans that you created. No matter how challenging things may become, continue to seek God's will for your life.

Intentionality

You will need deliberate action to follow God. God tends to bring people to a fork in the road – a choice will have to be made. When this happens, will you lean on your understanding or seek God's direction? Choose wisely because your choices will directly impact your home team. Your personal relationship with the Lord will have an impact on the rest of your team. It is the largest variable in your home team's success. Only expect your team to follow the Lord after you have committed to doing so.

Accountability

God always hold leaders accountable. The response of the team does not matter. God is primarily concerned with your obedience to Him as a leader. As a leader, you will be responsible for the decisions that you make and the actions that you take. Once God's will has been revealed, you will have to make a choice. Honest accountability is healthy for all great teams. Team members should lovingly hold each other accountable by encouraging each other to maintain a sincere relationship with God.

Order of Accountability

Leadership is glorified in our society. Many desire to be their own boss. Others have sought to become their own shepherds. Many people want to be leaders before they understand what it entails. Consider this: Teenagers often dream about the day that they will be large and in charge. They become tired of being bossed around by their parents and teachers. They dream of making their own decisions. They have no idea what they are really asking for until it is too late! Have you ever been there? If you are not careful, being in charge can create great responsibility and stress. Did you have similar ambitions as a youth? I sure did. Did the dream eventually match your reality, or did the dream turn into a nightmare?

The plans of man can tend to turn into nightmares, but God grants dreams of abundance. A dream is not the same thing as a vision. A vision provided by God is full of purpose and meaning. Dr. Tim Irwin seems to agree. "When thoughtfully formed and skillfully communicated, a purpose or mission provides motivation for the team. A great vision becomes a quest." (Irwin 122). The quest of pursuing a godly vision will originate from a quest of pursuing a closer relationship with God. God will always provide a mission that is bursting with purpose. Following the will of God, while forsaking your own will is always best.

Every family needs order, and every team needs godly leadership. Can you imagine how your job would be if there were no clear leader? Wouldn't that be chaotic? That team would be wild, chaotic, immobile and ineffective. Likewise, winning home teams need to become organized.

God has established an order of accountability. God has called for Jesus Christ to be the ultimate head of the family. God has required that husbands submit to the authority of Jesus Christ. This means that they are simply communicating to their family, the directives received from God. Husbands are called to act as ambassadors and orators for God, in the home. They should do so with love. God has commanded that husbands love their wives as Christ has loved the church. (Ephesians 5:25). As husbands demonstrate great followership of the Lord, this will enable them to become great leaders. Sometimes what husbands do, will speak louder than what they say. An old saint, named Eula Mae DeWalt, once told me, "The life that you live will speak for you". Husbands will do well to speak to the Lord more than trying to control aspects of the family. Humble yourself and know that the Lord is able to do what you are unable to do.

God has called wives to submit to their husbands, as unto the Lord. (5:22) Wives may not understand the directive at first, and they may not agree. Understanding may not be immediate. Paul refers to this structure as spiritual and mysterious. (5:32) Wives may have a husband that has yet to grow into being a great man. God still requires submission to their own husbands. God called the wife to follow the leadership of their husband, even if he has yet to develop into a godly leader. Sometimes the intercession of spouses will be more impactful than their words. Instead, she is called to be obedient to God by following her husband. Sin is not included in this equation. God hates sin and would not call any spouse to engage in it. Marriage truly begins to flourish when spouses learn to thrive, both as a follower and as a leader. Paul lays this out in his letter to the church at Corinth.

But I want you to understand that the head of every man is Christ, the head of a wife is her husband, and the head of Christ is God (1 Corinthians 11:3) ESV.

Human nature can make God's model tough to follow. Spiritual maturity is needed for husbands to become faithful team captains and followers of Christ. Spiritual maturity is also needed for wives to become faithful followers of their own husbands and Christ. Marriage truly begins to flourish when spouses learn to thrive in this design consistently.

Team Jewel
Leadership provides a great amount of freedom and peace when your life is guided by the Lord. Order creates freedom and not bondage.

Beware of Worldly Culture

Be careful not to allow worldly concepts to cause confusion within your home team. Sometimes, it is hard to recognize how modern concepts exist because sometimes worldly culture is mixed in with biblical concepts. Take a moment to ponder the following clichés that are often accepted by mainstream society.

My Wife is the Boss

Boss is probably not the best word to use in any relationship. A good synonym for boss is dictator. Even God is not a dictator. Consider taking the word boss out of your vocabulary. Team captain may be more suitable because it encourages teamwork. God has given humanity the opportunity to make decisions according to His counsel. God will encourage good choices, but He will not force you. If God does not act as a "boss," then no one on the home team is authorized to act as such. You will never hear me say that my wife is the boss. The marriage relationship is in really bad shape if anyone on the team is a boss. Why should you identify your wife as the boss when God has identified you as the team captain? This clearly goes against God's design.

Husbands, carefully watch your leadership. Your obedience to consistently follow God's design is important. Be careful not to allow your selfish desires to misguide you. As you follow the Lord, you will lead your family through green pastures. God will be glorified as a result, and your relationship with Him will flourish. Remember to pray for direction. Stand firm on the Word and share it to your family. Communicate to your home team with love and patience. They may not understand where God is leading the family, but your family will always understand that love.

Godly wives should not endorse this mindset either. Rejecting the leadership of your husband goes against God's design. Wives, encourage your husbands to stand as the captain of your home team. Encourage him to be the man that God has called him to be. Your words of affirmation will be like the wind beneath his wings. Tell him that you are praying for him. Tell him that you trust that he will walk before God in obedience. He may not be a great leader now, but your godly influence will have a major impact. Do not underestimate how much godly influence you have in your home.

The Neck that Turns the Head

Heads are unable to turn without the controlling muscles of the neck. This phrase refers to control. It implies that the neck does not mind the head being at the top because the head is still under the control of the neck. God did not ordain for wives to "control" husbands. God has also forbidden husbands from trying to "control" their wives. God has called for Godly leadership - not worldly management! Control is not part of God's design. Your words are powerful; please be very careful with them!

God has provided wives with a great amount of influence. This influence should be used to benefit the whole family and not just one person. Sometimes, wives have the intention of convincing

43

their husband to see something or respond a certain way. However, no one can turn a heart or change a mind. This is what God does best. God has granted you with one of the most powerful assets for your home team, intercessory prayer. Pray for God's will to be revealed and not yours. Then pray that God will guide your husband in that direction.

Happy Wife, Happy Life

There will be times in a marriage when spouses disagree. Do not be alarmed, this is perfectly normal. God has brought two people together that are very different. Spouses have different needs, desires, and perspectives. Spouses will only be able to please themselves and their family temporarily. The world has encouraged spouses to find happiness in tangible things that fade away. This could be money, children and possessions. These are nothing more than idols of the heart. Idols provide a temporary satisfaction but God is able to provide eternal happiness.

Husbands should not lose focus but instead, follow God to the best of their ability. They should listen to their wives and take their wisdom into consideration. Remember that God has not asked husbands to make their wives happy. Wives are not called to make their husbands happy either. Husbands and wives, pray for your spouse's joy regularly. Pray for your joy as well. Spouses that find their contentment in God, are joyful in all seasons. He is the only one that can give you true joy because people and things are fickle.

Healthy Phrases for Every Marriage

The previous phrases were worldly and unfruitful. Try some of these phrases instead:

What Can I do to Help?

Spouses usually appreciate support. The willingness to help and be a blessing, go a long way. This phrase will foster an environment of help and encouragement.

You Did A Really God Job with...

Words of praise will boost the confidence and morale of your spouse. Who doesn't like to hear words like this from time to time?

I Am Sorry

Hey, we all make mistakes. Be sure to acknowledge your fault quickly and ask for forgiveness.

Thank You Much, I Really Appreciate ...

If your spouse has done something that blesses you...tell them about it! It will probably put a smile on their face.

How Was Your Day?

Let your spouse know that you are interested in them. Maintain interest as they share the details.

We Make A Great Home Team

This is a positive affirmation. Everything may not be the way you like but perception is everything. This declares your contentment with your marital union.

Please remember that what you say will have a huge impact on your spouse. Choose your words wisely because they are powerful. Leadership and followership will be greatly influenced by the words that are used.

A Call to Focus

God summoned Abram from the tiny village of Haran (Genesis 11:31). It was small but was used as a highway to other cities. People were always passing through. There was an Aramean culture that had a huge impact on his spiritual life. Abram was surrounded by false gods as a result, Abram was surrounded by polytheism of cultures such as the Hindus, Sumerians, the Semites of Arabia, and the Egyptians, to name a few. The one true God approaches Abram in a world of idol worship. God introduces Abram to a purpose and the journey of a lifetime. Abram has to leave the familiar distractions of his past to pursue his purpose by focusing on following God.

Abram and Sarai also had to embrace the unique vision that God had for their home team. They were a normal family and seemed to be content with the life they had chosen. God disrupted their status quo and began to unfold a much greater vision. God makes a bold declaration to the couple,

> *"And I will make of thee a great nation, and I will bless thee, and make thy name great, and thou shalt be a blessing."* *(Genesis 12:2).*

Godly leadership and godly following, requires patience. Patience and focus are knitted together in great leaders. Abram needed to be at peace with not knowing when these things would come to pass. Abram needed to be okay with God's unorthodox timing. This seems like an unlikely time to switch things up. Abram was already 75 years old (12:4). As an old man Abram was called to abruptly leave his comfortable setting. Following God requires being comfortable with being uncomfortable. Abram had an opportunity to reach his blessed destination, but he and Sarai had to decide to make an immediate change. Abram's home team was now on the move.

A Call to Action

It was time to move. If Abram stayed in Haran with his family, he would not be able to apprehend the promise. God required that he act and do so immediately. Abram's initial faith in God was demonstrated through action.

> *Now the Lord had said unto Abram, "Get thee out of thy country, and from thy kindred, and from thy father's house, unto a land that I will shew thee." (Genesis 12:1)*

It is confusing to confess trust in God and not demonstrate it. Abram could have pondered this call for a few years, but delayed obedience is always disobedience. Moving too early is not helpful either. God's guidance includes also being aware of His timing. God's timing requires that you move when He says move, even when God's timing makes no sense.

That must have been gut-wrenching. Abram had to leave his extended family. The place where he spent much of his life would become a distant memory. He left the land with plenty of resources. Home was a place where he would have expected provision and protection. Now, he was called out to pursue a land that he didn't know. I wonder how he broke this news to the family that he would leave behind! I am sure his friends were convinced that he had lost it. The beautiful thing is that regardless of what emotions Abram was feeling at this time, he chose to act.

> *So Abram departed, as the Lord had spoken unto him; and Lot with him: and Abram was seventy and five years old when he departed out of Haran. (Genesis 12:4)*

A Call to Trust

In the beginning, Abram struggled greatly with trusting the Lord. It must have been tough to tell Sarai that they were leaving their home and he had no knowledge of where they were going. The author of Genesis does not record any words of Abram's wife, Sarai. If Sarai had asked any questions, Abram did not have any answers. That was the point. This was a valuable lesson from God. Both of them were learning how to trust God. Abram had to learn to trust in God's will for his family. When God chose Abram, he was a poor leader. He had so much to learn on his quest to follow God's vision.

Abram would not be an adequate leader until he first learned how to follow God. Abram's family was learning how to trust God by watching Abram trust God. This is true leadership. People learn so much by the actions of a leader. It is important to understand that things will probably not occur when or how you think they should.

I am sure that you and your spouse desire to have a successful home team. Abram and Sarai desired to have the same thing; Trust me, God wants you to have the same. Abram and Sarai had to trust God's design more than their own. God's plan points to a bigger picture – the picture of a winning home team. Trusting in God's plan glorifies Him and invites others to trust in Him as well.

God initiated dialogue with Abram. Abram had been chosen as a leader to walk before God. His whole household would be blessed as a result. Abram was leading his family, but he would be held responsible for his decisions.

A Call of Promise

Leadership demands responsibility. God has given Abram directives to follow, and he will be held responsible for his actions. You will see in future conversations that God will often go directly to Abram, the team leader. When things go well, Abram would be respected, and his name will be made great. However, this leadership also means that he would be held responsible when things do not go right. The good news is that the promise did not depend on Abram's responsibility, but instead, it was contingent on the faithfulness of God.

God has a rather large plan for Abram and Sarai. A large family will eventually exist from this union. God's plan was to establish a godly family that would exist in the future. The family had to come through a seed. God's plan was to have this family come from an old, ordinary and imperfect couple. Families of faith would come to look up to them. Husbands would come to learn faith by reading about father Abram. Wives would come to maturity by observing Sarai's model of growth. However, Abram and Sarai were afraid and unsure of what to expect.

> *Then the Lord appeared to Abram and said, "To your offspring I will give this land." So he built there an altar to the Lord, who had appeared to him. (Genesis 12:7).*

The offspring that God is foreshadowing of the Messiah came through that bloodline many generations later. It is foretelling of the many believers that would become part of the heavenly family through faith in Jesus Christ. The plan is much bigger than Abram can imagine. Be sure to know that God has great plans for your family. If you allow the Lord to lead your home team, it will have a generational impact! Some children and grandchildren will be thankful for the godly example through you. God's plan for your family is much bigger than you realize.

God promised that the seed would come from Abram and through Sarai. The beauty is that Abram could not receive this promise without Sarai. Likewise, there would be no promise without Abram. God revealed the need for each other. They would have to learn how to work together in order to receive the blessing that God had for them.

Team Jewel
If I win, my home team wins too. We will win together. We will rise and fall TOGETHER!

If you have some concerns on where God is leading your family, you are not alone. Abram and Sarai felt the same way. God will call you to greatness before you are great. God does not call those who are qualified. God instead specializes in qualifying those who He has called. You are not called to pursue greatness in selfish, worldly ambitions. Rather, God has called you to become the greatest servant of your home team. It shall not be so among you. But whoever would be great among you must be your servant. (Matthew 20:26). In the world, serving has gone out of style. Don't let that be true for your house, for it is the way of Christ. Your home team will become great, by learning to serve each other.

Husbands, do you fully submit to the authority of Christ. Do you allow him to lead you in all things? Please provide examples.

_____
_____
_____
_____
_____
_____

Husbands, do you have at least one mature believer that will pray for you and hold you accountable?

_____
_____
_____
_____
_____
_____

Wives, do you fully submit to your husband as unto the Lord? Do you truly see him as leader of the home? Please explain how your actions demonstrate this.

_____
_____
_____
_____
_____
_____

CHAPTER 2

TEAM HARMONY

"You can do what I cannot do. I can do what you cannot do.
Together, we can do great things."
–Mother Teresa

Mother Teresa's quotes signify that there is only so much that can be done individually. It highlights the need for a team. A winning home team will have to work together to succeed. God has designed the family to operate in harmony.

God's design for the family is visible in nature. Animals operate in harmony and put God's design on display. Animals of various species lack nothing by simply adhering to God's divine design.

The ecosystem consists of both predator and prey. Very few animals are at the top of the food chain. All animals must find consistent food for survival – most are the prey of another species. Things get chaotic in the animal kingdom; it is a sign that we reside in a fallen world. Most animals travel with their kind and tend to travel in groups to avoid becoming lunch for another species. Most animals travel in packs or herds; birds travel in schools. There are several reasons why animals travel together. Animals benefit from adopting a team concept and operating in harmony.

Wolves perform almost all of their activities in the company of other wolves. The wolf pack is usually structured as a family structure. The packs are led by the male and female wolf as well as the offspring. These packs can sometimes reach the high teens. Individual wolves have different roles. Wolves gather for social reasons and survival reasons like acquiring food. Most people would not realize that wolves also gather for their protection. As predators, wolves wisely travel in packs to ensure their safety and protection.

Dolphins travel in groups called pods. Super pods are formed and can reach up to a thousand members. Pods are formed for benefits of hunting, mating, and defense from dangerous predators in the water. Deepwater is home for some of the most dangerous animals. The survival of dolphins is solely based on their ability to exist in harmony with other dolphins. Dolphins do not have the large jaws or super sharp teeth. God did not design them to be predatory animals. Science identifies Dolphins as having high brain activity, but their success is dependent upon their community. The ability to live in community with other dolphins allows them to thrive in an environment that is unsafe.

Birds have always traveled in flocks. What is even more impressive is that they move in synchronization and harmony. Birds also seem to always be moving in the same direction without confusion. They travel with perfect spacing and precise timing. They possess an awareness that allows them to know when it is time to fly south for the winter. Birds typically form lines and V's, to take advantage of the aerodynamic factors that save energy. What is really impressive is that no matter how big the flock becomes; they still operate with discipline and organization. Birds do not operate in conflict, but instead, possess great harmony. While flying together, birds make impressive turns in the air without running into each other. Birds may not understand why they do what they do. However, these flocks thrive because they follow God's design of harmony and teamwork.

God's design for harmony is evident within the animal kingdom. This harmony is not always visible amongst humanity. God has also designed humans to live in community. If animals can live in harmony with other animals of the same species, why is it so difficult for humans to do the same?

Due to the introduction of sin through the fall, humans have struggled to live in harmony. The only opportunity for humanity to realize harmony again is to learn love from the Lord. Without being born again, sin and hate will run and ruin your life. The sin, within, is the greatest enemy. The good news is that Jesus has defeated sin so that we would no longer be slaves to it. The Christian faith is all about living in harmony with everyone and especially with the people of the household of faith (Galatians 6:10). The Bible speaks much about harmony within marriages. The Old and New Testament both speak on marital harmony. The Bible declares that two are better than one, (Ecclesiastes 4:9). God's design for your home team is to transform your home team by transforming you first. God has designed you to thrive with your spouse. All members of the family are blessed when the home team is in harmony!

Pursue Harmony

Instead of harmony, some pursue isolation and independence instead. God never said in His word that women need men. He never said that men need women. We only *need* the Lord. God said, "it is not good for man to be alone" (Genesis 2:18). This implies that it is not good for a woman to be alone either. Before Adam realized the benefit of having a helper, God was already at work in creating a suitable helper for him. Society has promoted division by highlighting our differences. God has encouraged harmony by exposing our similarities and celebrating our unique qualities.

Animals have enough sense to realize that things are better when they are not alone. Human beings are much greater than animals because we are made in the image and likeness of God. God has granted humans with the ability to reason. Unfortunately, sin has caused an impairment of judgment. God's design is for husbands and wives to depend on His guidance to navigate through life. Gender differences are by design. Do you and your spouse have the same skills, talents, and abilities? Your marriage will be at its best when you begin to appreciate and celebrate those differences, abilities, and roles. A harmonious home team sees uniqueness as an asset instead of a liability.

Pursue harmony by intentionally working with your spouse. There are times when husbands will need to delegate and defer to their wives and vice versa. God knows my efforts in doing this. There are valuable talents that Tasha possesses. Most areas where I lack skill or strength, the Lord has put in my bride. I also consider her to be a wise woman. I must admit that I enjoy observing God's work through her. I love to encourage her. I know that I can count on her prayers. I frequently consider her counsel when I need to make decisions because she sees things from a different set of lenses! Solomon makes it clear that you will be able to do much more with harmony. "Two are better than one because they have a good reward for their toil" (Ecclesiastes 4:9). A good reward will be the result when your home team has harmony. Even when married, it is important to fight against the urge to live in isolation and tension.

Musical Harmony

I am not the songbird or musician of the family. Don't get me wrong; I can carry a tune and sing to the glory of God. However, I know my limitations. It would not be best for me to join a choir. I'd rather hear my wife, who minored in music and has a beautiful voice. She has told me a few things in regards to music over the years. I consider her to be my music coach. Maybe I shouldn't say that until my voice gets better. Regardless, not all singers and choirs have perfect voices.

Excellent choirs need a few things. They must possess unity as well as harmony. There are other things that are needed for choir harmony. These two things are important because, within a choir, you have various types of voices and personality. The goal of the choir is to bring all of those differences together. An excellent choir has the goal of celebrating the uniqueness of the various voices but also to bring those voices together to become one unified voice.

Unity will stress the fact that even though there are various gifted and talented voices, it is important that the various voices become one. Musical unity allows for voices to maintain the same lyrics, tempo, and key. However, the individuality of each voice is still evident. Likewise, God has not called you to hide your unique qualities as a spouse but has called you to share them. Jesus stressed the importance of unity, "what therefore God has joined together, let not man separate" (Mark 10:9). God has given spouses the responsibility not to allow anything to interfere with this unity. With unity and the bond of love, your home team will stand strong.

Harmony is just as important as unity. Musical harmony requires for voices to blend. It may be a struggle to hear the individual voices within the choir because only the unified voice is heard. The voices may blend in so well that even when the ranges of the voices vary, they come together as one unified voice. It is possible to have unity but not possess harmony. Singing together does not mean that your voices are blended. One thing that is true for harmony is that each voice has to make adjustments to blend in with the rest of the choir. Likewise, God has called for spouses to harmonize together. They should be like-minded and on one accord.

If you plan to live in harmony with your spouse, it will require blending, mending and agreeing.

Blending

Marriage requires the willingness to collaborate. It requires each spouse to be willing to meet in the middle. It sometimes requires going completely to the other side to meet your spouse. The reality of blending is that you may need to sacrifice some desires to pursue harmony. Through marriage, God has brought two contrasting people together to become one.

And the two shall become one flesh. So they are no longer two but one flesh (Genesis 2:24, Matthew 19:5, Mark 10:8, Ephesians 5:31).

This truth is so important that it is quoted in four different passages. Fundamental mathematics teaches that one plus one equals two. This verse seems to imply that one plus one equals one! The Bible encourages a mental, physical, social and spiritual blending of two contrasting people. It sounds impossible, but with the grace of God, it can be expected.

Mending

Always remember that disagreements will occur and it is perfectly normal. What is most important is how you respond. A disagreement does not have to develop into a competitive match of verbal jousting. James provides some insight into the origin of division. What causes quarrels and what causes fights among you? Is it not this, that your passions are at war within you? (James 4:1). Spouses often become angry when their selfish desires and expectations are not met. Division can manifest in many ways. It can be expressed as anger, sadness, and anxiety. There can be physical, emotional, social and spiritual divisions that married couples experience. If you are dealing with marital problems, please refuse to allow division to linger. Reconcile with your spouse as soon as possible. Be intentional in doing so.

Agreeing

Agreeing - may involve agreeing to disagree. We may not always agree because of our different perspectives. Instead of focusing on what we do not agree on, focus on what we have in common. The prophet Amos explains the need to agree.

Do two walk together, unless they have agreed to meet? (Amos 3:3)

Sometimes, it is healthy to agree to disagree regarding minor matters. Disagreement with your teammate does not have to lead to division from your teammate. Spiritual agreement will aid in obtaining agreement in other areas. God desires for you and your spouse to walk in agreement, and His grace will make this possible. If you focus on communicating with God and your spouse, you will probably realize your agreements outnumber your disagreements. Ken Sande agrees with focusing on solutions instead of problems.

> *"When you speak to others about issues in their lives, be prepared to offer solutions to the specific problems you have identified." (Sande 181).*

You may not be able to agree on how or why the issue occurred. Shift your focus on solutions that you both can agree on. Place your energy on solutions instead. A solution-based focus will aid in preventing similar issues.

Harmony is Beautiful

When I first got married, I remember going out to eat with Tasha. I have no idea where we went, but I vividly remember the evening. I had worked up a large appetite, and I was ready to chow down. Tasha's warm smile demonstrated enjoyment. I was focused and eager to view the menu. I was considering an appetizer because I was starving. Tasha began to look at me from across the table and I was wondering why, but I decided to hold my tongue. She then asked me what I was going to order. I remember thinking, "why are you concerned about my order because I am surely just focusing on mine." I told her that I was unsure as I continued to observe the menu, even though I had a couple of things in mind already.

Tasha continued to investigate my order for the evening. After the third attempt, I grinned at her and asked, "why are you so concerned about what I am going to eat?" She said that she didn't know in a sweet little voice. When the waitress returned, Tasha placed her order and then I placed mine. When she heard me place my order, her eyes widened, and she said, "that sounds amazing!" I had hoped so because I sure was hungry. The waitress returned, and my prayers were answered. It was time to dig in! The entrees looked like something from a commercial and smelled even better. I remember the look on Tasha's face. She was salivating with excitement over MY plate. This was perplexing to me because this was my order and not hers. She seemed less than impressed with her order. When I began to dig in, she threw a question my way. You guessed it; she wanted to taste my food. In all transparency, I was not in the mood to share. At that time, I was not the sharing type.

This was over a decade ago. Tasha has taught me some things over the years. I have realized that if we go out to eat and I order a steak and baked potato, then that means that Tasha will also be having steak and baked potato that evening. However, if she orders shrimp scampi with pasta, that means that I have just inherited some good Italian food. I've learned to accept sharing my gifts with Tasha because she's willing to share her gifts with me. This allows us both to benefit and be blessed by the God-given gifts that we share. Even eating in harmony has been a joy and blessing to us.

Tension begins to build in the thirteenth chapter of Genesis. When Abram left his father's house, he did not go alone. Abram went with his household, Lot and Lot's household. God led them to a vacant land for them to inherit. It was not meant for both families to exist in the same land; some decisions would have to be made. Tension began to develop; the herdsmen began to allow the tension to grow into a dispute.

Take a look at the following figure, you see an illustration of the lack of harmony. The person on the left is facing and opposing the person on the right. They are thinking and saying different things. Two are not in agreement. This is a recipe for tension, confusion and stagnation.

Figure 1. Lack of Harmony

Tension is created when you see your spouse as an opponent and not as your teammate. Their herdsmen were not in agreement. Tension grew because the new land seemed too small to contain them both – this was by design. God did not intend to have both families dwell together in that land. This new season demanded choices and changes.

Now take a look at the next figure 2 on the next page. If you look closely, you should see a silhouette of both individuals on the same side. They are no longer opponents trying to win a silly debate. They are thinking and saying the same thing. They may not have started off being like-minded but they have come to an agreement in order to walk in harmony and work as a winning home team. Look at their words. Harmony tends to produce praise and worship in the family.

The goal of the Christian walk is to experience spiritual growth. As God blesses your home team, things will begin to change. Social and familial relationships that you previously experienced may not be ideal for the current season of your life. God may require you to leave familiar things to embrace new things with your spouse. This might include new locations or even responsibilities. Marriage is an adventure that is full of swift transitions. The beauty is going on this journey with God and your spouse. You never know where He will guide you, but you expect to be blessed because His will is best.

Figure 2. Team Harmony

Tension May Not Be Bad

Abram sensed the tension and demonstrated leadership by taking the initiative to resolve the conflict. He pleaded with Lot and requested not to allow the tension to grow but instead to dwell peacefully. He explained to Lot that they were family, they had a blood relationship. They were also spiritual brothers. They were trusting and following God together. Their commonalities far exceeded their differences.

> *Then Abram said to Lot, "Let there be no strife between you and me, and between your herdsmen and my herdsmen, for we are kinsmen" (Genesis 13:8)*

There will be days where you experience tension with your spouse. Regardless of the issue, remember to focus on the many things that you agree on instead of highlighting the few things that you don't agree on. Getting married may require you to take an inventory of your friends and family. Marriage will often require you to spend less time with folks from your past. It may simply be that the things you had in common have changed because God has changed you. When God is orchestrating change in your life, it is always good.

It is obvious that God was evolving Abram. Abram identified the main commonality of his relationship with Lot, and that was their relationship with God. Abram expected to be able to resolve the dispute due to what they had in common. He focused on what they had in common instead of focusing on the reason why they could not agree.

Celebrate Differences

Embrace the differences, see them as a great sign that is part of God's wise design. Disagreements may also occur within extended families. This is often due to certain expectations that others may have. Within the marital union, outside perspectives have very little value. If we are willing, God will surround us with mature believers, and He will speak through them. However, the couple must be in agreement with God. When the married couple stands in agreement with God, who can come against it?

Abram played peacemaker by encouraging reconciliation. He was focused on finding a solution and did not allow the problem to become a distraction. He could have easily focused on the problem or the differences they had, but instead, he focused on things that they had that would help them continue to operate in harmony. Up to this point, they have been traveling together and have had many things in common. They had the same culture, came from the same land, and had a long relationship. They now found themselves on the same adventure. Most importantly, they were following the same God. However, their relationship was still threatened with some tension. Abram presents the possibility of them separating and dwelling in different areas.

Is not the whole land before you? Separate yourself from me. If you take the left hand, then I will go to the right, or if you take the right hand, then I will go to the left." And Lot lifted up his eyes and saw that the Jordan Valley was well watered everywhere like the garden of the Lord, like the land of Egypt, in the direction of Zoar (this was before the Lord destroyed Sodom and Gomorrah). So Lot chose for himself all the Jordan Valley, and Lot journeyed east. Thus they separated from each other. Abram settled in the land of Canaan, while Lot settled among the cities of the valley and moved his tent as far as Sodom. (Genesis 13:9-12)

Abram allowed Lot to choose instead of demanding the land that he wanted. Abram was the senior member and Lot's uncle. God has been leading him directly and not Lot. Abram instead chose a path of humility and sacrifice. Lot chose a nice area to settle, and Abram went to Canaan. Both lands were part of the blessing. Please remember that sacrificing your desires and focusing on what your home team needs is righteous. God will honor your obedience. God will keep you and bless you, just like He did Abram.

After Abram's act of love and self-sacrifice, God reminds Abram of the covenant promise that He was establishing with His servant. The Lord said to Abram, after Lot had separated from him,

> *"Lift up your eyes and look from the place where you are, northward and southward and eastward and westward, 15 for all the land that you see I will give to you and to your offspring forever. 16 I will make your offspring as the dust of*

*the earth, so that if one can count the dust of the earth,
your offspring also can be counted. (Genesis 13:14-16)*

The first thing that he said is that they were family. Abram did not allow the dispute of the herdsmen to become a dispute between him and Lot. They also were good friends. Abraham was not willing to throw all of that away because of a silly argument between someone else. However, the situation called for them to make some quick adjustments and decisions.

Likewise, you have to examine the relationships that you have in your life. God has called for intentionality in making your relationships work. Communicating with honesty and consideration will often lead to harmony. Abram said they were brothers. That was a two-fold statement. Although they were not brothers having the same mother and father, they did share a blood relationship. You should always be able to keep harmony with other members of the household of faith.

They had land before them. They could have focused on the issue at hand, but it made much more sense to focus on the fact that there was a blessing right in front of their eyes. The Scripture does not say what the dispute was about. Based on Abram's response, it can be assumed there was a dispute over the blessing and how it would be occupied. Abram suggested that there was enough for all of them to be blessed. Abram knew that disharmony was not God's will.

Team Jewel
Make it a big deal to celebrate any blessings that God sends to your home team. Make it fun and encouraging. Find things to celebrate. Always display gratitude.

Abram suggested that Lot should occupy one territory with his family and Abram's family would occupy the other side. It seemed to be a very reasonable suggestion. It was not a suggestion that would bless Abram only, but it was a suggestion that would bless everyone involved. Both Lot and Abram were blessed as a result.

They were practically neighbors. Zoar and Canaan were close in proximity. Not only were they neighbors, but they were living in harmony.

When there is tension with your home team, the Lord encourages swift reconciliation and love. However, tension with extended family and in-laws do not hold the same level of importance. For the sake of harmony, it is sometimes better to allow a little space. Abram enjoyed some privacy, and this may prove to be a blessing for your marriage.

You may have a situation where you have relatives or even in-laws that are not willing to endorse your union. You have to do whatever you can to guard your marriage and avoid toxicity. Stand with God and your mate, be eager in pursuing harmony with your extended family. However, be relentless in guarding the harmony of your home team primarily. God has made it clear that your household is your primary responsibility. Love your in-laws well. Listen to God's declaration, "Therefore a man shall leave his father and his mother and hold fast to his wife" (Genesis 2:24; Mark 10:8).

Separation is not the focus of this passage but instead to put your marital relationship above your relationship with others. The passage also emphasizes holding fast to your spouse. Holding fast means to be firmly secure. Invest in a marriage that is built on a solid foundation so that it can withstand any challenge. Invest in having a marriage that is secure and rooted in Jesus Christ.

Stand against confusion and anger. This is Satan's design and not God's. "For God is not a God of confusion but of peace." (1 Corinthians 14:33). Satan's comes to divide and confuse. God's design is peaceful. Protect the blessed home that God has provided. Always love, but it may have to be from a distance. The worst thing that you can do is to separate from your spouse to maintain past relationships with friends or relatives. This is not God's design, and it will cause great resistance within your marital union.

Team Jewel
The Biblical principle of leaving and cleaving is very helpful. It will help you prioritize relationships. Keep your relationship with the Lord as number one. The relationship with your spouse needs to be next. Allow nothing to disrupt those two.

In what areas, do you see your spouse gifted, and yourself struggle? Identify three areas.

_____
_____
_____
_____
_____

When have you recently worked as a team with your spouse to accomplish something or complete a task?

_____
_____
_____
_____
_____

CHAPTER **3**

TEAM COVENANT

"The only chains you should wear in life
are the chains of commitment."
—Shannon L. Alder

Shannon Alder's quote emphasizes the necessity of commitment. A team covenant needs to be adopted and practiced by all members of the team. The team covenant acts as a guide, and the ability to follow it will prove helpful. Captain Chesley Sullenberger had to rely on safety procedures and progressions that he learned through his years of flight experience.

In 2009, Sullenberger experienced the unthinkable. Due to bird-aircraft strike hazards, he had to deal with double engine failure. This would make a violet crash imminent in most circumstances. He was able to make swift decisions that would eventually save his life, the life of his crew and the passengers. Without any firm place to land the plane, he had no choice but to land the plane on the Hudson River.

God's grace was clearly involved. Captain Sullenberger possessed great instincts and the ability to think in high-pressure situations. He also was able to rely on the standard flight training. He worked through various progressions and emergency procedures during the emergency. Without flight standards, landing the plane would have been impossible.

In general, these flight standards are pretty standard across the industry. Other things are very specific within each company. Captains have to submit to very rigorous training. The training takes place regularly and is a requirement to continue employment as a pilot. Aviation companies seek to make sure that all of their pilots are well trained and equipped to go out and do their jobs extremely well. Various things take place during this time of training. Certain things are emphasized to ensure that the pilots are fully prepared.

These aviation professionals are also introduced to new trends that may impact their ability to do their job with excellence. If certain trends and vulnerabilities have the potential to cause difficulty, it is the company's responsibility to make their employees aware. The objective is to minimize exposure to mistakes and dangers. These are preventative strategies that have worked well. In aviation, safety and quality control are essential.

Emergency procedures are thoroughly covered in trainings. As a result, aviation is one of the safest means of transportation. It is still important to make sure that the pilots are reminded of what to do in case of an emergency. If you don't know what to do and a dangerous event occurs, all passengers will be in danger. Captain Sullenberger was prepared for an emergency because of the preparation and standards in the company flight manual.

It is important that all employees understand current emergency procedures, especially the pilots. Passengers and members of the flight team trust in the leadership of the pilots. They oversee all phases of the flight trip. The staff and passengers look to them to command authority and to lead them safely to the destination.

Expectations have to be communicated and fully understood by the whole flight team before take-off! All organizations usually have an operation manual. The aviation industry uses a document called the

FOM - The flight Operation Manual. Pilots have several manuals that they have to internalize. In case of an emergency, pilots have no time to pull out a manual! The FOM acts as an organization covenant that creates common ground for the flight team. The whole flight team benefits from having a uniform document that creates clarity and understanding.

Uniformity is a Blessing

Thank God for the exhaustive and intensive training because passenger's lives depend on it. It enhances safety and success. The flight teams are organized, and the same should be true of your home team. What about your marriage? When things get difficult, what is the first thing that you turn to? Has this been clearly communicated to all members of your home team? Airlines use a FOM. Sports teams use playbooks to call plays. Christian home teams should use the Bible to prepare for a life that contains challenges.

It is not if, but when. Storms tend to find the home team. Be intentional to have the Word of God before you regularly and not just when tough times come. If you are consistent here, you will not be weak and troubled when tribulations find you. When you meditate on the Word of God day and night; you will be like a tree planted by the rivers of water, that bear fruit in all seasons (Psalm 1:1-3). Be proactive to connect your home team to the Lord regularly.

Team Jewel
Establish a regular devotion time for your home team.

Learn the Playbook

The home team should have the Bible as the team's playbook. Couples should get their directives from the spiritual command center, which would be heaven. Whenever the pilots or the team captain begins to stray away from the tried and proven techniques within the FOM, danger will be imminent. Whenever families begin to stray away from the proven Word of God, their connection to God will fade and communication will become full of static. A decline from God is not something that happens overnight, but it's a slow drift.

In this world, your home team needs a plan! There is an abundance of divine knowledge and wisdom in the Bible. However, it is through prayer and a relationship with God that home teams know how to navigate through life. You must stay in communication with air traffic control from heaven. Nothing can be hidden from God. He possesses all knowledge and vision and is more than able to guide your family. The success of your home team depends on it. God's plan is to be the primary navigator of your home team.

Team covenants are essential to provide clarity. A covenant is a binding commitment between two parties. Typically, in contractual law, there are conditions for each party to fulfill for the covenant to remain intact. There's something that each party must contribute for the contract to remain binding. The covenant involves those two parties and no one else. If one of the parties does not fulfill their end of the bargain, then the covenant is nullified and is no longer binding. Within a covenant, expectations for each party are set. In godly marital covenants, there are three parties. That includes both spouses and the Lord.

People rarely follow through on what they intend to do. The team covenant is not about perfection. You will make mistakes; members of your home team will do the same. Team covenants are about effort, change, and intent. The team covenant should outline the most pertinent principles by which your home team will live by. God has ordained order and structure. No matter how hard you try to meet expectations, you will come up short. Be at peace knowing that Jesus Christ was perfect where you have failed. He was perfect so that you would not have to be. Now that is good news!

Order is good. Rules are a necessity. Without order, chaos will be the result and disorder will create confusion. There may be a general commitment without clear expectation. There may not be a real consistent commitment to the Word. Sometimes, home team members have alternative expectations, so clarity and communication are paramount. Establish a covenant of principles between your spouse and God. These will be the guiding principles of your home team. It is good to put the principles up so that all team members can see them. This resembles the directives given by God to Moses and eventually to the Israelites before entering the Promised Land.

And thou shalt bind them for a sign upon thine hand, and they shall be as frontlets between thine eyes. And thou shalt write them upon the posts of thy house, and on thy gates. (Deuteronomy 6:8-9)

Team covenants must be established between three parties. It must be established between husband, wife, and God. A threefold cord is not easily broken (Ecclesiastes 4:12). The team's playbook is the Bible which is sufficient with all knowledge necessary to thrive in your marriage. God will grant you wisdom on how to apply these principles in your home team.

Take a look at the following figure 3 that shows an example of the Towns Home Team Covenant. This is a list of principles that Tasha and I have incorporated. Notice that each principle has a correlating scripture with it as well because it is our foundation. You can have as many or as few as you would like. The goal is to allow these principles to help you establish the culture in your house.

Figure 3. Team Covenant

Team Jewel

Take time to sit with your spouse. Pray and study the Scripture together. Let God lead you to identify foundational principles that your home team will adopt. This may take several days and weeks but continue to do so until you have these principles documented.

Create a Winning Culture

All great teams have an organizational culture. It would be very unwise for a company to wait until it hires all of its employees and then decide to adopt its foundational principles. It wouldn't make sense for a sports team to go through tryouts, play a couple of games, and after consecutive losses decide to adopt foundational principles.

Likewise, it would also be very unwise to choose a spouse, get married, have children and later decide to adopt principles to create a family culture. These principles are the foundation that your home will be built upon. The culture at that point would already be established. Every marital team has a culture. Some cultures are toxic, and some are healthy. When houses are built, the foundation is laid first. If you desire to have God lead your home team, a team covenant is needed. Having a clear vision for your home team will be an absolute blessing.

Trust in the Process

During my senior year in high school, I had a basketball injury in which I injured the ring finger on my right hand. I dislocated it and used a splint as the doctor directed, but I was not willing to wait. I decided only to skip two games before I took the splint off and began to play again. I know I seemed impatient. I wanted to play so bad, so I took a risk. I mean, I couldn't allow my senior year to go by and miss the last half of it due to a finger issue. So, I completed that season and later realized that my finger was damaged and never healed correctly.

I should have exercised patience by allowing it to heal properly, which may have only been another two weeks. The injury would have initially healed itself, but now, because I did not allow it to heal fully, the only way to fix it would be through surgery. The healing process would have to start over. It was risky for me not to follow the doctor's orders. This time, the process would not just be a few weeks, but it will now take several months to heal. It pays to follow the doctor's orders. Likewise, it pays to be patient and to trust in the process that God has for you.

Establish a Culture for Your Home Team

Anyone who has played sports on a high level realizes that sports can be very strategic and cognitive. The playbooks can also look like encyclopedias. Each member of the team is required to learn and fully know that playbook before they can take the field and play. The likelihood of the coach calling every single play in the playbook is very slim. The Bible is God's playbook. It is full of wisdom that would take more than a lifetime to learn. Athletes are challenged to learn all of the variations in their playbook. Likewise, if you desire to be strong in your faith, you should spend as much time learning the spiritual playbook as well. Athletes then have to go to practice and games to demonstrate their ability to run the play. Home teams have to also learn to apply God's word to their family culture.

Team covenants should contain the most pertinent principles from God's playbook and it should be used to create the core culture. These principles will be most critical for your home team. These are not intended to be merely wall décor; the goal is to apply them. If your marriage is new, a team covenant will be an exciting exercise. If your marriage is struggling, establishing a team covenant should be refreshing. One thousand scriptures recited are not nearly as powerful as two that are applied! The Word is able to transform your marriage and make it brand new.

Couples often describe where they are struggling but have no understanding why. Some have failed to identify biblical principles by which they should live and help them establish that culture. If asked individually, it is likely that each spouse has a different set of principles and values. The struggle occurs when there are no clear expectations, responsibilities or principles to follow. Success in marriage is obtained by consistently and proactively following Christ.

The real question is - are you willing to change? Are you willing to acknowledge that you do not have it all figured out? Can you honestly say that your design for your home team has not been successful? If there is a willingness, the Lord is able. If the culture is sick or toxic, both spouses have to work together to allow a godly culture to be created.

Create a Balance

Balance is essential. Working to provide for the family is important. Check as many of the boxes that you can. There are many spouses across the nation that work extremely hard to hold different aspects of the family together. Be reminded that you will consistently miss perfection. That is fine. Take a deep breath. Relax. Put your trust in God's strength instead of your own. Rest is biblical, and it is godly. God has extended grace to you, go ahead and receive it. Release yourself from the bondage of trying to be a superhero. It is refreshing for couples to balance it out with spending time together to enjoy themselves. God is a God of balance. If you are tired of striving for perfection, listen to the words of Jesus Christ.

> *Come to Me, all you who labor and are heavy laden, and I will give you rest. Take My yoke upon you and learn from Me, for I am gentle and lowly in heart, and you will find rest for your souls. For My yoke is easy and My burden is light (Matthew 11:28-30).*

When dealing with the human body, there is something called pH balance. The soil of the earth also has a pH balance. The goal is to read it by a particular scale. The pH can be very acidic or toxic, or it can be very alkaline. If there's too much toxic acid in it, then the culture is bad. Too much alkaline will be harmful as well. It is best to be in the middle of that scale for nutritious growth. If you want to have healthy fruit come out of that soil, you must first change the soil's environmental balance. Healthy marriages must also be willing to have balance by avoiding the extremes of too much work. A balanced life is conducive for producing spiritual fruitfulness. Move out of the way and let the Lord water the soil of your heart.

Team Jewel
Incorporate a weekly time of rest. Consistently set time aside to spend with your spouse. Be okay with saying no to anything that tries to interfere. At the core of marriage is the relationship with your spouse. Keep it strong and guard it with a balanced lifestyle.

God's Chosen

God established a covenant with Abram. The Bible does not explain why God chose Abram. Obviously, it had nothing to do with Abram's qualifications. One of the first things God said to Abram was not to be afraid. God addresses his fear that was antagonizing his faith. God makes it clear to Abram that He is aware of his inner battles. Abram wants to have faith in God, but his fear had been overpowering him. God makes it clear that he does not need to be afraid, but He will be his protection and shield.

Sometimes, God will grant the vision before He provides the resources. The main resource that Abram needed was faith. Abram reminds God of the promise, but he brings up the fact that he does not have a child. God explains that the promise will surely come through him. Abram began to speculate if God will use his servant instead. God again ensured that it would come through Abram. Abram had faith, but it was small and inconsistent. Have you been there?

However, there is not much evidence of his belief. His faith was demonstrated in his words because he asks God for a sign. Then, his words began to articulate his thoughts. Abram responds by asking God a question. "And he said, Lord God, whereby shall I know that I shall inherit it" (Genesis 15:8). Without much evidence to hold on to, Abram's faith is beginning to expand. Abram was a man of very small faith, but he was still chosen.

God's Covenant

God initiated and held together the covenant with Abram. On one side of the covenant, there is fearful and imperfect Abram. On the other side, you have a holy and righteous God. God had given Abram a promise. God had promised to hold up all the responsibilities of the covenant. God also promised to provide the seed. God even provided an abundance of land. God promised always to protect him and God granted increased his faith as well.

God can be counted on to fulfill His responsibilities of the covenant. He always follows through on what He says. There's never been a time that God has not followed through on His promises. Unfortunately, when God establishes covenants with His creation, mankind always fails to fulfill their end of the bargain. The good news is that this is a unilateral Covenant. The covenant with Abram was unconditional and one-sided. God would bring it to pass with the responsibility of Abram. Abram was unable to break it. Jay Adams explains the nature of biblical covenants. "The binding nature of the divine covenant assures them that divorce is not an option. That is a wonderful difference that Christians possess. The covenant is a lifetime commitment." (Adams 24) God does not break covenants. He willingly brought His promise to pass and honored His covenant, in spite of Abram's failures. This covenant was going to be brought to pass regardless of what Abram did. If a successful covenant depended on Abram, failure would have been the result. Thanks be to God that He upheld the covenant and blessed Abram beyond his many faults.

God will do the same for your marriage. I am sure you try hard to be a perfect spouse and parent. The reality is that you do not have the capability of being a super spouse. It is important to set reasonable expectations. Do not expect perfection from yourself or your spouse; only God is perfect. Put your trust in Him. In spite of your failures, God will strengthen the covenant of your home team.

God's Righteousness

Abram was not righteous. He was guilty of lying and seeking his own interests consistently. Due to the faith granted to him by God, he has been counted as righteous before God. Abram was not perfectly righteous. "And he believed in the Lord; and He counted it to him for righteousness" (Genesis 15:6). There was nothing righteous about Abram, but God counted him as righteous because of his initial faith.

Abram repeatedly lied as a result of his fear. Abram has been a poor leader, and he allowed the emotions of his wife to guide his decisions. This also was out of fear and a lack of trust in God. Regardless of why he did what he did, Abram still missed the mark repeatedly. Abram was unworthy of such an honor, but God still used him.

Missing the mark should be expected. People are more capable of failing than succeeding. There should be no pressure. We are victorious in Jesus Christ. (1 Corinthians 15:57) Sometimes, you won't have enough arms, eyes and time to do what you feel is needed to support the home team sufficiently. Always remember that Abram failed God long before you did. Once you recognize that you failed, ask for forgiveness from your spouse and God, and get back to serving Him the best way that you know how. Be okay with recognizing your own weakness and God's strength.

Team Jewel
Take time to analyze team expectations that exist between you and your spouse. Be accepting of mistakes and shortfalls. Be careful to be verbally affirming of your spouse. The world has a way of creating unrealistic expectations. Be the strongest encourager on the team.

At the beginning of Abram's mission, he made some terrible mistakes. The beginning of his journey screams failure. Success seemed far-fetched, but there would eventually be a numberless multitude that would refer to him as Father Abraham. It seemed unlikely that he would be a pillar of the faith. It is not about how you start, but instead, it's about how you grow and live for God. If God can do it for Abram, He can surely do it for you.

The Bible is the document that all couples and families should follow. It is a proven guide for all family success. However, couples need to have principles or (team jewels) that are known by all members of the home team. The principles should be biblical and should guide our everyday life. The law of the Old Covenant contained 613 laws. However, the 10 commandments have always been a general guide of life for believers. Families should follow all the guidance found in the new covenant of Christ. However, there should also be specific principles that guide their culture as a family.

Team Project

Sit down with your spouse and pray for guidance. Identify a group of biblical scriptures that you both hold as extremely important for the family. Explain why they are important to you. Write the final principles with supporting scripture on one piece of paper. Put it up somewhere that the home team can be reminded. This exercise will require teamwork; it will require corporate prayer. Once you have completed the exercise, sit down with your children and communicate those that are of age. Allow these team jewels to guide your life daily. Begin journaling these down below.

_____
_____
_____
_____
_____

CHAPTER **4**

STICK TO THE SCRIPT

"Sometimes, you can't see the road ahead, but as you keep going, it gets clearer. Stay the course as the fog of life dissipates."
—Sanjo Jendayi

Sega revolutionized the gaming industry with their introduction to the Sega Genesis. With a great enhancement of graphics, video gamers all across the world fell in love with the console and Sega sold many of them. Sega became a household name with iconic games such as Sonic the Hedgehog which rivaled the popularity of Mario Brothers! Kids enjoyed unlimited hours of fun with these popular games. Soon after that, companies began to develop counter options for consumers. One of those was Sony PlayStation. Sega came up with the idea to redevelop the Genesis and come up with a better version of it called the Sega Dreamcast. It was not an improvement of the original console, but it looked totally different from the original one. The modifications were so extreme and advanced that it failed to win the hearts of the gaming community and the loyal customer base developed years ago. As a result, the Dreamcast failed to live up to the billing of the original Sega Genesis. The company should have stuck to principles in the original plan.

Microsoft is one of the biggest brands in the world. Through innovation, they have changed the way people use computers. They have revolutionized how companies do business. Individuals have changed the way that they look at the personal computer because of Microsoft. The technological world as we know it, was forever changed because of Microsoft. Microsoft took the industry by storm with the launch of Windows. It was fresh, efficient and very user-friendly. It was unlike anything else that had been created. However, Microsoft began to launch a new version of Windows every single year with the goal of making each version better than the previous one. The annual anticipation was massive. The company's market share and notoriety continued to grow year after year. However, things changed with the release of Windows 8. It was a highly acclaimed release. Unfortunately, it did not live up to the hype. There was one change that was made that created challenges for the company. Microsoft was known for being the best at creating software that was easy to use. The Windows 8 adaptations upset a lot of customers because innovations were supposed to make things easier but created confusion. Major complaints ensued. A new version had to be released immediately, in order to salvage customer satisfaction. Microsoft should have stuck to what had worked for them in the past.

The best corporations are always seeking to be innovative. Being ahead of the competition is what business is all about. Companies know that they are not the only ones that try to gain market share. Some designate teams for the sole purpose of sparking innovation. Sometimes, changes are made in order to roll out a new initiative. When adjustments are made, it is important to stay connected to the core values of the establishment. However, the adjustments come across in new initiatives with the goal of enhancing success. If these corporations are not careful, modifications can actually stunt success.

Sega and Microsoft learned to stay connected and stick with what works. All teams need to learn to exercise much care and wisdom before making major changes. Change within the home team is inevitable. Just as corporations have to be careful with their changes, married couples have to do the same. Modifications should be Holy Spirit inspired and bathed in prayer. Changes need to align with the culture and guiding principles of your team covenant. God has a divine design for your home team, and it will include some surprising changes. The best thing that you can do is follow His design without deviation.

Take Your Time

Corporations sometimes make swift adjustments in logistics or sales. Sometimes they succeed and sometimes they don't. Corporations do not loosely make changes in the organization. This usually involves focus groups, research, and major changes. With all of the preparation that is made, it is still possible that things will not go as planned. You never know how the public will receive things. They need also to be aware of what other companies are doing in the marketplace. It is best to handle with care.

Swift transitions to the original plan are not always healthy. With anything in life, when we are rushed, we tend to make mistakes. Knee-jerk reactions only consider the immediate moment. When decisions are made in haste, remember many of them cannot be undone. They tend to have long-term implications. What the world calls mistakes, the Word calls sin. Sin is very destructive to every aspect of life. It will stifle your relationship with God and impede a winning home team. Most families have good intentions and high expectations. If God has led your home team by providing a vision and a plan, then it would be wise to trust the Lord's plan to all the way to the end.

Some transitions are minor adjustments, and others are major changes. A major change might include having a child, changing a job or serving at a different church. Minor adjustments might include a change in your work schedule or deciding on a family vacation in the summer. If the Lord is truly the head of the home team, it is righteous to allow Him to guide both the large and small things in your family. It is truly peaceful to allow God to lead. Stress is removed because He is providing direction. Put the stressful load on His shoulders instead. The world often tends to speed up the pace and to create stress. Listen to the encouragement that Paul gave to the church at Philippi.

> *Be careful for nothing; but in everything by prayer and supplication with thanksgiving let your requests be made known unto God. And the peace of God, which passeth all understanding, shall keep your hearts and minds through Christ Jesus. (Philippians 4:6-7)*

Paul suggests that the best way to handle anxiety is to fight it with prayer. It often begins with a surprising and emerging issue that demands attention. You have no way of controlling the existence of these issues. They are just part of life. However, with God's grace, you can control how you will respond to them. Paul does not say bring only the stressful things in prayer. He suggests bringing "everything" to the Lord in prayer. This is followed by a promise that the peace of God will maintain the desires of your heart and the thoughts of your mind. In the stressful world that we live in, choosing to allow Jesus to keep your heart and mind will prove to be a blessing.

God is known to make swift transitions with home teams. God's changes rarely make sense at first. However, they always work out in the end. It is important that we are fluid and flexible in allowing God to make adjustments whenever He sees fit.

Team Jewel
Change is good. Just make sure that God is leading the change. If He is, do not resist but embrace the newness.

Minimize Trust in Self

The mindset to avert from proven strategies often comes from overconfidence. It is impossible for you to lead your family better than the Lord. Our ideas are always inferior to His plan. "There is a way that seems right to a man, but its end is the way to death." (Proverbs 14:12) These plans seem to work initially, but over time, they lead to destruction. Some things unfold slowly. Overconfidence in self is nothing but pride. Pride can be like cancer that attacks marriages. The Bible declares that "pride comes before the fall" (Proverbs 16:18). Teams that go into a game with too much confidence in their ability, can sometimes be humbled by their opponent. One necessity of all sports is always to respect your opponents. The truth is on any given day, your opponent can beat you. It is good to have confidence in your team and to believe that your team is better than the opponent, but you also need to have confidence in the strategy that your coach provided. Trusting your coach's plan is to trust your coach fully. If you do not trust your coach's plan, then you probably have pride lurking within.

Eliminating pride and implementing trust is needed for every home team. It is not possible to both trust God while maintaining pride in your heart. Pride will separate you from your spouse and hinder your relationship with God. Intentional humility is needed to antagonize pride. If you never see your faults or struggle to admit fault, then you are blinded by pride.

God has a specific plan for every home team. Home teams are at their best when they fully trust in the plan that God has provided. Sometimes, home teams will follow God's plan for a short season, experience success, and then begin to do their own thing. Freestyling and shooting from the hip will lead to destruction. There's no need to reinvent the wheel when God's plan always leads to success. If this is you, allow Him in the driver seat of your heart. Let Him lead you today.

Trust in God's Outcome

God's design requires faith. He has never failed. His will and His way are perfect all of the time. It is in your best interest to follow God's divine plans very closely. Trusting God requires living a life of faith. It requires doing things that may not make much sense. It requires regularly reading His Word. Trusting the Lord requires laying down your will in order to embrace the will that He has for you. A life of faith is about serving the Lord instead of serving yourself.

If you've never fully trusted Him before, you are missing out on an adventure and the opportunity to fully depend on Him. You will miss an opportunity to see Him work powerfully in your life. God will not force His way into your life. Instead, God wants you to choose to allow Him into your life and home team completely. It is possible to be a Christian who faithfully attends church but still block God out of the most intimate aspects of your life. God is just asking for you to fully allow Him into your life and into your marriage.

Follow God's Instructions

Moses was chosen as a leader for the children of Israel. However, he did not always follow the Lord's instructions. Whenever Moses walked in obedience, God faithfully blessed him. Israel traveled in the wilderness and needed water. Look at God's instructions to them.

> *Take the staff, and assemble the congregation, you and Aaron your brother, and tell the rock before their eyes to yield its water. So you shall bring water out of the rock for*

them and give drink to the congregation and their cattle
(Numbers 20:8).

Sounds pretty simple right? Well, Moses ignored sound judgment
and decided to deviate from the clear plans that God provided. His
obedience had proved to be profitable in the past, but Moses could
not seem to help himself.

> *And Moses lifted up his hand and struck the rock with his*
> *staff twice, and water came out abundantly, and the*
> *congregation drank, and their livestock. (Numbers 20:11)*

This was clearly not a time to try innovation. God had faithfully kept
Israel safe in Egypt. He had faithfully brought them out safely.
Moses should have continued to trust and obey the Lord. Things
seemed to be perfectly fine because the congregation was still able
to quench their thirst with the waters of Meribah. However, this
disobedience was a costly one. His present thirst was satisfied, but
his sin produced future consequences. Due to the disobedience of
Moses' generation, was not granted access by God, into the land.

Weakening Faith

Home teams will always operate at their best when they closely
follow the voice of their heavenly coach. Abram and Sarai sought to
follow His voice as well. Abram and Sarai found themselves trying to
hold on to the promise that God gave them such a long time ago.
They were both struggling to hold on like an enduring match of tug-
of-war. However, Sarai was experiencing great anxiety. In their
culture, it was very important for women to bear children. Children
were greatly valued, and the woman's worth was attached to the
children she birthed. She was already old when the promise came,
and now she is really old, yet still without a child. Time seems to be
running out. It was the perfect opportunity for Sarai to take matters
into her own hands. Unfortunately, that is exactly what she did.

Sarai's Weakness

Sarah's faithlessness was demonstrated by her inability to wait. She became full of anxiety. Her biological clock was way overdue, and she was tired of waiting on the Lord. Furthermore, she probably struggled with an identity crisis by focusing on the approval of others. God's approval is most important. The blood of Christ has provided this approval. There is no question if God approves of you because the blood of Christ has granted that. You just have to receive the fact that you are approved of the Lord. There is much our society can learn here. It is liberating to live for the approval of the Lord only. Living for the acceptance of others is way too tiring. Free yourself and cast down the idols of your heart.

Sarai should have focused on being approved by God instead. This fear and anxiety come to life with a dangerous suggestion. Sarai suggests that Abram sleep with the Egyptian servant. This may have seemed rational to Sarah because Abraham needed an heir. She acted in direct opposition to what God had promised. Sarai resented that she has failed to become pregnant with the heir of the promise. It seemed to her that God had raised the expectations with a miraculous promise but had failed to deliver.

> And Sarai said to Abram, "Behold now, the Lord has prevented me from bearing children. Go in to my servant; it may be that I shall obtain children[a] by her." And Abram listened to the voice of Sarai." (Genesis 16:2)

This seemed to be factual on the surface. Would God really play with Sarai's emotions by promising something that He did not intend on producing? To Sarai's defense, bearing a child was probably one of the most important things in her life. Her emotions must have been all over the place! Her anxiety meter was on 1000! This promise probably consumed her thoughts both day and night. Anxiety and anger were mounting in her heart. The years are fleeting and time is no longer on her side.

Remember that God's timing is not the same as yours. She decided to no longer wait on God and to take matters into her own hands. She creates her plan and strategy to help God's will come to pass. Sarai had tried to undermined God's knowledge and power. Her emotional distress led her to move in confusion. Sarai should have been more patient and faithful. God did not restrain Sarai from bearing. It was just not yet her season! When God promises you something, remember that He will do it in His timing. Remember that It may not be God's will for you to act on it right now.

Abram's Weakness

Abram did not put up much of a fight either. Abram was dealing with his inner struggles; his fear. He also seems to be trying to please his wife. Pleasing his wife disrupted his relationship with God. Hindsight is always clearer, but Abram should have rebuked his wife and decided to obey God instead. The mark of a true godly leader is to follow the Lord faithfully regardless of the opposition. Abram was far from modeling such righteousness. Likewise, husbands will need to follow Christ faithfully and without apology. Do whatever you can to come to an agreement with your spouse but be a leader by coming to agreement with the Lord first.

There are many things that he could have done in this situation. Since Abram was supposed to be the leader, he could have reminded Sarai of the promise that God gave. He could have sought counsel from God even though he already knew what God promised. In this situation, the worst thing that Abraham could do was hearken to the voice of his wife because she was not hearkening to the voice of the Lord. Sarai was listening to her flesh and emotions. What Sarah suggested was purely out of emotion and was not rational at all. It was definitely not Spirit-led. Abram failed to hearken to the voice of God and encourage his wife at this difficult moment.

Years before, Adam made the same mistake, and all humanity had to pay for it. Instead of walking in obedience, he disobeyed God with little or no resistance. One impulsive decision of disobedience led to years of painful consequences.

> *And to Adam He said, "Because you have listened to the voice of your wife and have eaten of the tree of which I commanded you, 'You shall not eat of it,' cursed is the ground because of you; in pain you shall eat of it all the days of your life." (Genesis 3:17)*

God gave Adam a very simple plan. Adam failed to follow God as the emotional suggestion of his wife influenced him. God held Adam responsible for not leading his wife properly. He followed his wife and failed to follow God. They failed to stick to God's original plan.

Team Jewel
Listen closely to your spouse but obey God. Be careful not to allow your emotions to guide your decisions.

Abram and Sarai had dwelt in Canaan for 10 years when Sarah had offered this proposition. God could have granted the heir within that time frame. They were already old and in their 80s. However, God wanted to make sure that the promise that He gave, would only be possible through Him. Abram and Sarai cannot take credit for this situation, but instead, they had to point to God as the only way for them to bear children while being close to 100 years old. Sarah had a plan to satisfy her flesh and address her anxiety. God had a plan of blessing them, obtaining glory and bless future generations that would follow Him. We are at our best when we embrace our God-ordained role of glorifying God.

> *And Sarai said to Abram, "May the wrong done to me be on you! I gave my servant to your embrace, and when she saw that she had conceived, she looked on me with contempt. May the Lord judge between you and me." (Genesis 16:5)*

In order to be a recipient of God's promise, you need to stick to God's plan. God only revealed pieces of His plan to Abraham and

Sarah. The problem was that they tried to fill in the gaps. Please remember that God does not need your assistance to accomplish His will for your home team. God only requires obedience and faith. One of the wisest statements recorded in Scripture was by the mother of Jesus. At the wedding at Cana, they were trying to solve the problem of running out of wine. Mary gave simple but sound wisdom. His mother said to the servants, do whatever He tells you. (John 2:5). If you desire to have a winning home team, it would be wise for you to do whatever God tells you. It takes wisdom to understand that God's plan and wisdom are so much better than yours.

It was not a sin for Abram to lay with Hagar because it was lawful. The sin that Abram and Sarai committed was the disobedience and lack of faith that they both had in their heart. Their decision was in direct opposition of God's will. God will always reward faith. Paul declares these words in Hebrews, "Without faith, it is impossible to please God." (Hebrews 11:6) God is pleased when home teams decide to trust Him during what seems like faithless situations. Unfortunately, the problem was made worse by casting blame on each other. Both Abram and Sarai were at fault, but both were trying to blame the other without taking responsibility. Excuses never amount to anything, but both Abram and Sarai tried to use them anyway.

Do you truly believe that God's will for your family is best? Do you feel that your spouse does as well? Explain.

_____

_____

_____

_____

_____

CHAPTER 5

KEEPING THE SCORE

"Be kind to one another, tenderhearted, forgiving one another,
as God in Christ forgave you."
—Ephesians 4:32

Paul's words to the church at Ephesus, clearly present the mandate to forgive. True forgiveness will include kindness and tenderheartedness. The responsibility to forgive comes from the reality of God's forgiveness towards us. The following historical account demonstrates that as well.

In 1957, Curtis Mitchell documented a New York Crusade which was led by Billy Graham. It was considered to be one of the most astounding evangelical crusades because of the reputation that New York had. New York was known as a vile city at the time. Before this movement, God had used the evangelist mightily, and lives were transformed as a result. Due to New York's reputation, many did not believe that God would be able to move in such a dark place. Many declared that the city was too far away from God to be reached with the gospel.

Graham followed the call in-spite of the naysayers. He worked diligently with his ministry team, various churches in the city and other leaders. They prayed without ceasing. The goal was to work together as a godly team in order to witness the transformational power of the Gospel. There was a lot of time, prayer and resources invested in the project. The Crusade went on for months and nightly packed the Madison Square Garden. As a result of all of the prayer and concerted efforts, a miracle took place in Manhattan that summer. An estimated 56,000 decisions were made for Christ. Of those, 22,000 were under the age of 21. Over 2,000 people were college students from the New York area. An estimated 96 million people viewed one or more of the 14 Saturday night TV broadcast from the garden. The average nightly attendance at the Garden was over 17,000. Few believed that God's light would be able to penetrate such a dark place. The majority was wrong. That is why Curtis Mitchell's book is entitled "God in the garden."

This is a display of what can happen when teams work together and submit to the guidance of the Lord. After the Crusade was completed, Billy Graham received thousands of letters explaining how people were blessed by viewing or attending the crusades. What was encouraging is that the letters received were from adults who explained why they decided to follow Christ. Many reported that their marriages were restored as a result. Billy Graham's message was very consistent. It Involved repentance, love and following Jesus. Many of those who viewed the crusade found themselves in troubled marriages. Many were contemplating divorce. God had transformed them, their spouses, and their marriages. Thousands of marriages that were on the rocks were restored after spouses made a commitment to follow Christ together. They decided to grant forgiveness to their spouses because Christ had forgiven them.

Listen to a few of the testimonies:

From Rhodhiss, North Carolina - "We listen and see your program every week. I have received a blessing from them. My husband and I were thinking of separation, but since your revival, we have been drawn closer to each other." (125)

From Union, North Carolina - "Before your wonderful sermon last Saturday night, my husband and I were about to give up. Our marriage was just about on the rocks. We were constantly bickering and quarreling. We had discussed seeing a marriage counselor. During your sermon, God spoke to each of us in a wonderful way. Immediately after, we went into our bedroom, got down on our knees, and gave our hearts to our God. Thank God our marriage is saved." (125)

Who is Keeping Score?

In sports, scorekeepers have the responsibility to keep time, statistics and the score. They sometimes make mistakes but are usually good at working together to produce fairness and accuracy. Athletes are sometimes not fully aware of such details because they are focused on competing. Athletes should leave statistics to the coaches and focus on winning instead. Likewise, spouses should leave keeping score to God.

God loves to use the past as a positive learning experience. Your experience will not be wasted. God can teach you life lessons from the good and bad of your past. There is a new set of principles and ideologies that will be in place. Couples make a very big mistake when they try to incorporate all of the principles that they learned from their parents and bring them into the new relationship. Even if you come from a blessed Christian home, God intends for couples to seek Him first when starting a new home team. Respect the home established by mom and dad, but judge everything by the Word. God wants you to obtain fresh revelation from Him by seeking His face through study and prayer.

Having a balanced perspective will bless your home team. It's not healthy to always dwell on the past, neither is it good to always look to the future without growing from your past. Be aware of misconceptions and fear that you have brought from previous relationships. Some individuals are missing a blessed future due to the inability to be delivered from past relationships.

It can also be very damaging when the person is always looking towards the future and never considers what God has brought them through. God will often guide you to the rearview mirror so that you can see all of the valleys and mountains that He has brought you through. These moments should expand your confidence in God. No matter how difficult things may be or become, God is able to change things around. Just remember that change first begins with us. If He brought you through it before, then He can surely do it again.

Team Jewel
God will use your upbringing as a learning opportunity. He will call you to incorporate some of those solid principles. Ask your parents for guidance and prayer. Go to them after you go to the Lord and your spouse. Seeking advice does not require that you incorporate it.

Prioritize What is Most Important

It may be hard to see your parents as sinners saved by God's grace. Before knowing God, most believers looked up to parental figures. It is normal to want to become like your parents. It is a blessing if you still hold your parents in very high regard. Having a strong love toward them is godly. The problem is when the love for parents is exalted above the love for your home team. Nothing should ever exceed your love for God. Always keep God at the center of the home team. Parents and extended family members are usually good at giving advice.

Sometimes, the fondness of parents will overflow into talk with spouses. The rhetoric may sound something like this: When I was a kid, I did this. Or my mother used to cook this. When I got sick, my mother used this. Be very careful with your words. By always referring to your childhood home, you can sometimes put pressure on your spouse to try and duplicate the same. It's okay to talk about how great your parents are and how much you respect them, but while you do that, make sure that your appreciation of your parents is not turning into idol worship. Love them well but don't worship them. However, be very careful of what expectations and culture you carry with you into your marriage. Jim Estep seems to agree:

> *We carry into a marriage the expectations we received from our own family, and sometimes they are in conflict with one another (Estep 31)*

It is godly to talk about how much you love and respect your spouse. It is great to do this publicly. It is great to do so around your family as well. Use words like this: "My wife does a great job of fixing good healthy meals. My wife is a great trustee of our finances. My husband is a great provider and works hard." Expressing your appreciation of your teammate is pleasing. Tell your spouse how much you appreciate God bringing them into your life. Take their words into consideration and prayerfully listen but allow your conversation with your spouse and God to have the final say. I've always said to my wife that if we agree with God on something, no other approval is needed!

If you are not careful, your words can create competition between your parents and your spouse. Words have great influence. They can create great harmony or a major divide. Where does your loyalty primarily reside? First seeking an outside source about dislikes and challenges at the home front is a big mistake. Instead, bring these issues before God first. God may direct you to also communicate them openly to your spouse. God might also guide you to seek external guidance from a spiritually mature friend. Just having a listening ear is not enough. It is always good to have someone who will lift you up in prayer while keeping information confidential. It is not mature to bring things to a friend before first bringing them to your heavenly coach.

Forgive Quickly

Remember that your spouse will miss the mark. You have to realize that you will make mistakes. We all are capable of failing to live up to standards and expectations. You do not have enough arms, eyes and time to accomplish the many responsibilities of being a spouse and parent. Abraham and the other historical characters in the Bible failed as well. Abram and Sarai failed repeatedly. When you fail to forgive swiftly, the offense has an opportunity to take root in your heart. Things begin to linger and lead to other problems.

Once you recognize that your spouse is guilty of something, address the infraction with the Scripture as your guide. Then, be quick to forgive them and reconcile. If this is hard for you, it may be helpful to consider your faults first. If you have missed the mark, ask for forgiveness from God, then ask your spouse and get back to being a winning home team. Winning home teams are not perfect, but instead, they are sound at resolving conflicts biblically.

Forgiving is not easy. Biblical forgiveness is highly unlikely without the empowerment of the Holy Spirit. It is not in human nature to be forgiving. The sinful nature desires to hold grudges. However, following Jesus Christ requires forgiveness. Jesus explained in His word the reason why Moses was permitted to allow divorce. It was because of the hardness of their hearts (Matthew 19:8). Jesus explained that this was not according to God's original order for marriage. There are only a few conditions in which a divorce should be granted according to the new covenant in Christ, and it should be a last resort.

The hope of the gospel is to receive a new heart that is soft and not hard towards the things of God. God promised that His New Covenant will provide a new heart that can love and forgive. Without receiving this new heart through faith in Jesus Christ, the spiritual maturity needed to forgive is not accessible. Forgiveness of the heart is an act of God that takes place within the hearts of those who are born again. Dr. Willie Richardson explains this well. "The person who is converted and growing spiritually can love the way God loves. God's love practiced in the family is what makes a wholesome family. A spiritual person is a loving person. The unregenerate heart is just not capable of loving others. Unfortunately, self-centeredness is the default result.

The beauty of the Gospel is that God grants you forgiveness and has commanded that you forgive your spouse consistently. Jesus explains how many times you should forgive before giving up. Jesus said to him, "I do not say to you seven times, but seventy-seven times" (Matthew 18:22). What you have freely received, be willing to give freely. There is nothing you can do to earn your forgiveness, so do not try to make your spouse earn it. Forgiveness is a form of grace, and it is free. Unforgiveness will lock you up in a spiritual holding cell of your past. When you let go, you are setting yourself free to experience the life that God has ordained for you to have.

Couples need to resist the urge to keep score. Continue to wipe your mate's slate clean through forgiveness. Forgive them as Christ has forgiven you. Forgive and refuse to bring up old transgressions. If we are not careful, we will begin to keep score against our spouse is an enemy or an opponent. When you do this you and your spouse both lose. Your home team will continue to struggle until you learn how to operate as a team. Look at the following figure.

Figure 4. Team Scoreboard

Be Aware

Skill is required in driving automobiles. There is a reason why testing is necessary to drive cars legally. All teenagers are eager to get their opportunity to grip the steering wheel. Parents are often hesitant because of the great amount of responsibility that it brings. The government is aware of the dire statistics regarding driver safety. To minimize these statistics, a thorough process of standardized testing is in place. If teenagers can pass the written and practical tests, they will be able to obtain their permit. After months of successfully driving with another licensed adult, teenagers gain the liberty to drive alone with a license. Teenagers every year are giving the grave responsibility of safely driving a two-ton vehicle. The amount of responsibility is enormous.

Awareness reigns supreme in safe driving. My mother once gave me this wise quote, "it is not only about you driving well, but you have to be very careful and aware of the reckless drivers that are on the road." We are unable to control the reckless drivers around us, but we have to be aware of what is going on around us. Focus only on what you can control.

Safe drivers use mirrors to help them maintain awareness of their surroundings. God wants you to focus on the road ahead. Sometimes, God desires for you to look in the rearview mirror to see what has happened in the past. Learning from your past can allow you to learn from past mistakes to avoid repeating them. Sometimes, it is even encouraging to look at past successes to give you faith for the current season of life. The rearview mirror may be a tool to view the poor choices of the past. That may cause you to be more cautious in the future.

Some people are just unable to let go of things that someone did in the past. It is impossible to move forward when you are bound with the chains of unforgiveness. It is very hurtful to be on the receiving end of a grudge-holding spouse. Holding your spouse in contempt does not make much sense. Grudem warns against hypocritical self-righteousness:

> *"When I'm self-righteous, I'm saying that your sin against me is ultimately more serious than my sins against God, but Scripture is clear. Because we are the most forgiven people in this world, we should be the most forgiving people in the world." (Grudem/Rainey 202)*

Following God requires letting go of the past and living in the present. Moving forward requires forgiveness. Unforgiveness is bondage. However, forgiveness will allow you to move on and move forward. Many marriages are stuck in the past because the spouses are unable to forgive or forget what their spouse has done. True forgiveness means that you will not bring up your spouse's mistakes in the future. Forever keeping your spouse's failures in front of them is an example of keeping score.

Team Jewel
Forgiveness is a blessing, but unforgiveness is bondage. Read the parable of the Unforgiving Servant (Matthew 18:21-35)

Team Project

Search your heart for anything that you have been holding against your spouse. Write these things down. These may be known or hidden. Have your spouse do the same. Identify things that you have failed to forgive yourself of and communicate these things to your spouse. Pray together for strength to let go of the past. Since God has forgiven you, willingly forgive each other.

Abram and Sarai's Faithlessness

Abram and Sarai really did it this time. Their conspiracy was historic. God had blessed them with a mission, resources and a covenant relationship. How did Abraham and Sarah repay God? With willful disobedience. They were guilty of trying to sabotage God's plan. It is important to remember that Abram and Sarai were still loved by God. However, selfish sin has ruled in their hearts. Sarai and Abram make a selfish suggestion that would impact others besides themselves.

> *"And Sarai said to Abram, "Behold now, the Lord has prevented me from bearing children. Go in to my servant; it may be that I shall obtain children[a] by her." And Abram listened to the voice of Sarai" (Genesis 16:2)*

It seems as if God's plan has been destroyed. It is wonderful to know that the fulfillment of God's plan does not depend on us. Abram eventually concedes to his wife. Hagar conceives Abram's son, Ishmael. Even though Sarai suggested this arrangement, the result seemed to touch her at the core. She is not full of contentment, but instead, she meets Abram and Hagar with strong resentment.

"And he went in to Hagar, and she conceived. And when she saw that she had conceived, she looked with contempt on her mistress" (Genesis 16:4)

Sarai led this revolt against God's plan, and now, she is immediately bothered in her heart. To make things worse, Abram fails to show any consideration for how Hagar must have felt. Abram fails to take responsibility for his part in the situation. Both Abram and Sarai are responsible for the mess that was created. Unfortunately, innocent people have been hurt as a result. An innocent woman and an innocent child have endured pain because of their faithlessness. It is not uncommon to generate plans that seem sound and clever at the beginning. However, plans apart from God's plan will always come to ruin.

In your marriage, you will also make terrible mistakes. There is no mistake that you can make, that God is not aware of. He has literally seen it all. It is important to observe God's response. He handles the situation with great wisdom and love. God handles this situation the same way that spouses should handle each other. God could have issued a strong rebuke to all parties involved, instead, He decides to respond with grace and patience.

God immediately cares for the Egyptian handmaid and her son, Ishmael. God is extremely compassionate to her. She was caught in the crossfire. Hagar unknowingly and unwillingly has been put in a very difficult situation. She now finds herself homeless with a newborn child. There is no father in the picture because Abram seems to detach from the situation. God makes way for her to return to the place from where she left. Fortunately, she would return with a promise from God.

The angel of the Lord also said to her, "I will surely multiply your offspring so that they cannot be numbered for multitude." (Genesis 16:10)

God made a promise to Hagar. God was extremely gracious to her, when no one else was. The promise that she received sounds similar to the promise given to Abram. God promised to bless Ishmael even though he was not the child of promise. Abram now has a blended family. He has one child with Hagar but will have to wait years before Sarai conceives.

Abram and Sarai were guilty of having selfish ambition. The decisions made had nothing to do with glorifying God or loving their neighbor. An innocent woman and child are hurt as a result. Frustration and confusion are aroused. This was totally avoidable.

God's Faithfulness

God could have come with fire and brimstone. He could have scolded them to express His disappointment. God could have chosen another family. God was well aware of what they would do but decided to use them anyway. What God does next is a great demonstration for married couples. Consider this: God makes no mention of their sin. They are well aware that they have made a big mistake. Sarah even mentioned it in the text (Genesis 16:5). Sarai was anticipating God's judgment. They may have expected to have the promise revoked. Surprisingly, God fails to bring it before them. He fails to even mention their sin.

Time is continually running out. Abram and Sarai have yet to receive the promise. To make matters worse, they have attempted to take matters into their own hands. Abram is now eighty-six years old. (Genesis 16:16). The promise seems unlikely based on their age. Now, the promise seems very unlikely due to the major sin that was committed. God shows himself faithful to Hagar but fails to address Abram or Sarai immediately. You might have expected God to say no or to punish them. Instead, God is quiet toward them. He ministers to the mistress and begins to clean up their mess.

Team Jewel

Remember that God does not go back on His promises. You cannot control when He moves or how but remember that God is faithful. He always does what He says.

We can learn from this passage that God does not go back on His promises. He is a God of His word. He is a God of integrity. He is a God of forgiveness. Believers are called to attempt to model these same godly characteristics to others.

God could have brought the list of infractions before Abram and Sarai. God knows all but decided not to even address them. Consider the covenant relationship with your spouse. God knows the score. He's well aware of the statistics. God knows of your actions, your worldly thoughts, what you have done and failed to do. However, God does not dwell on past failures. He does not continually bring up your wrong. God does not bring up how much you owe Him. The truth is that God has been good. The Bible says that all good things come from above (James 1:17). Anything good in your life can be attributed to God's blessing. You should respond with a great deal of gratitude. Express the same type of graceful forgiveness to your spouse. Be compassionate just as the Lord has been compassionate toward you.

So, what about you? Do you have godly perfection? Have you ever done anything wrong against your spouse? Maybe your marriage is one-sided as well. Are you the only one that is positively keeping it together? Does your spouse need to straighten up and get their act together? If you are thinking these things, this mindset is contrary to God. If God can overlook the faults of Abram and Sarai, then you should be able to overlook the faults of your spouse. God was perfect in the covenant relationship and still chose not to bring up their past mistakes. God only reminded them of the promise. Be careful with your words. Forgive your spouse quickly and be reminded of the promise that you made to each other.

Do you struggle to forgive your spouse fully? Do you struggle not to remind them of their past mistakes? Why? And How?

_____

_____

_____

_____

_____

CHAPTER **6**

MATTERS OF THE HEART

"But God shows His love for us in that while we were still sinners,
Christ died for us."
—Paul of Tarsus; Romans 5:8

Paul's words to the church at Rome explains what true love is. God demonstrated love through Jesus Christ so that we could fully understand what love is about. Love can be manifested in many forms. Love is often caught instead of taught, like the story below.

One of the best love stories that I know of was not introduced through the cinema screen. It was not something that I read about nor something that I heard about. I had the honor to witness it with my own young eyes. I have often heard the saying, seeing is believing. Even though I saw it, I did not truly understand what I had seen.

Way back in 1943, a young American Soldier by the name of Joshua Stanford Towns went into World War II to serve his country. He was a soldier secondarily. Joshua was primarily a servant of Christ and servant-leader of his home. He was known to send love letters to his wife. He proudly took the risk of possibly not having the privilege of seeing his bride again. He marched on to serve his country in spite of that possibility. He served his country overseas, in spite of the racial challenges he faced on American soil. He fought in the war. However, he also had to fight for racial equity as an employee. Due to the melanin in his skin, he fought hard for the basic respect of being a man and citizen of the United States of America. He fought for decent wages and good life for his family. The need for mental, physical and spiritual strength was already part of his young life.

Joshua was a quiet man who didn't speak much. He instead was great at leading by example. He faithfully served his church, Greater Salem Baptist Church in Louisville Kentucky, for decades as an usher. For many years, Joshua demonstrated what love really meant because he lived a life of sacrifice.

The story shifts to a weary Joshua. He was now overtaken by fatigue and aging. Joshua is no longer a young man who was able to run like the wind. The vibrant energy of a soldier had left him. His mind was no longer able to contain information because it had been struck by dementia. Joshua's memory had faded, and his personality was non-existent. He had served his family, served his country and served the Lord while in his youth. Now the time has come where he needed to be served and retire from his labor as a great leader.

Due to many ailments of aging, his three daughters sought to hire a CNA, to provide much needed help at home. A determined voice quickly spoke out against this idea. Joshua's wife Loretta Australya Towns took offense to the suggestion of the family. The lady that he loved and served for years had something to say. Loretta stood only four feet 10 inches tall and weighed a little bit over 100 lbs. She was adamant that no outside help was needed! Their daughters could not do much to change her mind. The matriarch of the family had spoken. She demonstrated her love by sacrificing in order to take care of her husband, the same way that he sacrificed to take care of their family for many years. Their marriage was not perfect, but their love was strong like flint rock.

I was privileged to witness Loretta take on the duties of a CNA even though she had no official training. Loretta was not totally healthy either. Loretta struggled with emphysema, but tired lungs and limited oxygen did not stop her. She battled early stages of Alzheimer's, but the love of her husband was fresh in her mind. After fending off her loving daughters, Loretta took on the daily responsibilities of caring for her husband. Her girls pitched in to help but their mother did not leave much left to do. To this day, I still do not understand how she was able to bathe him, dress him and feed him.

The romance had faded but the love of God had abounded much more. Loretta was an old woman, with a weary body. However, she faithfully served the Lord by faithfully caring for her husband when convenience and comfortability was nowhere to be found. Joshua served the Lord by caring for his bride and family as long as he could. Loretta glorified God, by serving her husband, until death overtook him. He was 83 and Loretta became a widow at age 78. Loretta passed away 5 years later and joined her lifelong friend as a citizen of Heaven. I know not of a better image of what love is and these images have been engrafted in my mind for years.

The greatest love story ever is that of Jesus Christ, the great husbandman who redeemed His bride from the bondage of death and slavery, by willingly dying in her place. He washed His bride with the living water and provided her every need. Jesus Christ became known as the suffering servant who proved His love by serving through tribulation that led to death. The above story is a valiant effort to emulate the sacrificial love demonstrated by God the Son, Jesus Christ. The Towns' Home Team succeeded in modeling true agape love and glorifying God in the process!

So, What is Love Anyway?

Love is "a willing commitment to the welfare of another person, treating them as Christ treats me." The world already does an exceptional job of promoting the love of self. Mankind already inherits what we know as self-love. However, the Lord is encouraging the love of others and to love others as themselves. The world would be a better place if people considered the wellbeing of others before their own. Your marriage will be transformed when you and your spouse begin to consider the needs of each other first.

Love is not sex, romance or infatuation. Love is not something that you trip over and fall into. True love is everlasting and without conditions. In order to possess real love, you have to go to God. Jesus said, "by this shall all men know that ye are my disciples, if ye have love one to another" (John 13:35). You cannot know or demonstrate real love without knowing God. This is because the Bible declares that, "God is love." (1 John 4:8)

The Bible gives a crystal-clear description of what love looks like. Paul gives us a "Love Litmus Test" in his letter to the church at Corinth. "Love is patient and kind; love does not envy or boast; it is not arrogant or rude. It does not insist on its own way; it is not irritable or resentful; it does not rejoice at wrongdoing but rejoices with the truth. Love bears all things, believes all things, hopes all things, endures all things." (1 Corinthians 13:4-7) Do you believe that your spouse is able to see some of these qualities in you? If the answer is no, there seems to be a deficiency of love in your marriage. Let us explore love a little further.

Learn Authentic Love

Authentic love is sacrificial. You may not be called to physically die for anyone during your lifetime, but the Bible calls for all Christians to die to self. The apostle Paul explained this call to die, "I protest, brothers, by my pride in you, which I have in Christ Jesus our Lord, I die every day" (1 Corinthians 15:1). Believers are called to deny themselves their desires and choose to pursue what Christ desires for them. Jesus told His disciples, "If anyone would come after me, let him deny himself and take up his cross and follow me" (Matthew 16:24). Every Christian is called to take up their cross and follow Christ. True love is about self-denial. You will be best able to love your spouse by having a willingness to die to your self-centered desires.

True love demands sacrifice! Loving your spouse through sacrifice glorifies God. I understand that this can be difficult at times. However, denying yourself to pursue the Lord's plan for your life will bless your spouse. If you follow the Word, you will be fully empowered to love your spouse truly. Love within your marriage needs consistency and should become a lifestyle. It then must become something that you incorporate into your marriage. In a Christian marriage, sacrificial love should become second nature. Here are four ways to show love to your spouse.

Articulate Love

Love needs to be articulated. This is something that can be difficult for men. Some men might have a hard time expressing themselves emotionally and putting into words how they feel. It is important that both spouses articulate their love for each other. Be careful not to coerce your spouse to verbalize their love. You want it to be something that comes from their heart. Try to avoid extreme repetition in verbalizing your love to your mate. Remember there are other means of helping your spouse knows that you love them. There are few quotes of Jesus articulating His love for others.

However, the Bible is full of verses that clearly present the Lord's passion for His bride. Here is one in Revelation.

> *Behold, I give of the synagogue of Satan, who profess themselves to be Jews, and are not, but rather, they lie behold, I will make them come and worship before your feet, and to know that I loved you (Revelation 3:9).*

Jesus promises to reward the true believers who proved their love and loyalty by being obedient. The Lord's love for the body of Christ is undeniable. Be sure there is no doubt in your spouse's mind, or anyone else's that you love them.

Demonstrate Love

Love also needs to be demonstrated. It's important that our emotions lineup with our demonstration. They often do. The problem is when your emotions and heart are contrary to the Word of God. Emotions are often contrary to biblical commands. It is unwise to trust emotions because they are fickle. Your heart can be deceiving as well. Love is proven when you put your selfish desires aside to be a blessing to others. Love is not a noun only. In Scripture, it is often used as a verb. Jesus was persistent in demonstrating His love for us. Consider John's words,

> *"By this, we know love, that he laid down his life for us, and we ought to lay down our lives for the brothers. 17 But if anyone has the world's goods and sees his brother in need, yet closes his heart against him, how does God's love abide in him? Little children, let us not love in word or talk but in deed and in truth." (1 John 3:16-18)*

It is impossible to question Jesus' love for you. Jesus did not verbalize his love often, but His demonstrations were numerous, and they spoke loudly. There was no better way for Jesus to prove His love for His bride than to die willingly for all. He perished so that you and I may have eternal life.

Reciprocate Love

Give love as it has been given unto you by God. Reciprocated love is something that is commanded to all believers. It is not uncommon to try and prove love for God while forsaking to love your neighbor. God does not identify this as authentic love. God makes it clear that we best reciprocate our love for Him by walking in obedience. Our obedience to God is demonstrated in our love toward others and especially our spouses. Your love for your spouse will prove your love for the Lord. Look at what John said.

> *"Beloved, if God so loved us, we ought also to love one another. No man hath seen God at any time. If we love one another, God dwelleth in us, and His love is perfected in us."* (1 John 4:11-12)

The Lord demands believers to reciprocate their love to Him, but not by expressing it back to Him only. The Lord requires that love is expressed to your neighbor as proof that you really love Him. True love for Jesus Christ is all about obedience, and His command is to love your neighbor. There is no closer neighbor to you than your spouse. The apostle John explains further,

> *If anyone says, "I love God," and hates his brother, he is a liar; for he who does not love his brother whom he has seen cannot love God whom he has not seen* (1 John 4:20)

John explains that it is impossible to love God but hate your neighbor. There is no grey area with love. If it is not love, then by default, it has to be hate. The previous text explains hate as refusing to love. When you are a follower of Christ, you are then empowered to love unconditionally. Each believer must pray for strength and decide to obey. The Word states that if we think we love but hate even one brother or sister, then we are liars. Your love for God and your spouse will be real when you reciprocate the love that Jesus Christ gave to you by denying yourself.

Perpetuate Love

Lastly, love must also be perpetuated. Inconsistent love is not real love at all. Love is not something that you have one day and lose tomorrow. Inconsistent love is confusing and is emotionally driven. There's no such thing as falling out of love. True love is eternal. Be careful to continue to love regardless of what someone has done or said, show love to them anyway. Wouldn't you want someone to love you regardless of your faults? The love that Jesus Christ displayed was authentic and consistent. It was not contingent on our actions. His love did not wait on reciprocation. The apostle Paul boldly proclaims:

> *"For when we were yet without strength, in due time Christ died for the ungodly. For scarcely for a righteous man will one die: yet peradventure for a good man some would even dare to die. But God commendeth His love toward us, in that, while we were yet sinners, Christ died for us." (Romans 5:6-8)*

No matter your background, nationality or economic status, everybody has a heart. The question is what do you have a heart for? Who do you have a heart for? The heart contains our desires and passion. The problem is that love is often wrongly prioritized. If your heart is not primarily toward Christ, your heart is misguided.

> *Finally, if he determines to glorify God, he will be less likely to seek or demand from her what only God can provide. He will be satisfied with and by God, and he will simply seek to serve his wife." (Grudem/Rainey 203)*

Spouses that love the Lord more than their home team has a heart this is guided rightly. The heart represents what we love the most. Consider these three stages of caring for your heart.

Assess the Heart

The world has often advised us to follow our heart, but the Bible says that the heart is untrustworthy. "The heart is deceitful above all things, and desperately sick; who can understand it?" (Jeremiah 17:9). Be careful to analyze your heart and compare it to God's Word. How do you know what is in your heart? Pay close attention to your words. Listen to what the Lord said, "for out of the abundance of the heart the mouth speaks." (Matthew 12:34b). People rarely say things they do not mean. Pray for clarity and the Lord will assist you in assessing your own heart. You might be surprised by what your heart contains.

Cleaning the heart is similar to cleaning a dirty closet. You might put it off because it is so junky. You might even be fearful of what is in there. If you never address the closet, the junk and funk will never go away. Assessing your heart will take great courage and faith.

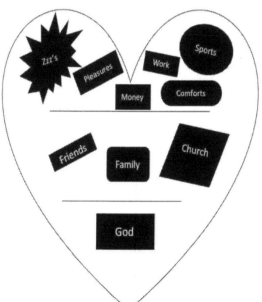

Analyze the Heart:

- Cluttered
- Wrongly Organized
- Selfish

Figure 5. Cluttered Heart

If you fail to assess your heart, over time it becomes cluttered with unnecessary things. Does Figure 5 resemble your heart?

Purge the Heart

Once you have identified the desires and priorities of the heart, some are healthy, and others are toxic. Some are healthy but are wrongly prioritized. Anything that opposes your relationship with God, needs to be cast away. This is where accountability will be fruitful. Be sure to share these things with your accountability or prayer partner. You will need someone to pray and challenge you to truly leave these things in the past.

Many years ago, I participated in collegiate athletics, so I loved sports. When I got married, I still had a fondness for basketball. I was aware that marriage brought new responsibilities but didn't expect conflicts. Well, Tasha brought it to my attention that I was spending more time away than she would have liked. I did not see it at first, but I considered her words. God began to work on my heart. There were advantages such as cardio and health. However, my time should have been used more wisely. I realized that my cardio health through competitive basketball needed to have less of a priority. Years have passed since I have joined any competitions. It was a sound decision because what God is building through my home team has much more priority in my heart. God will also lead you to draw a line in the sand.

Prayer and fasting are very effective in conditioning the heart. Sinful desires often take root in the heart like weeds. You will have to starve them. What do you have in your life that is feeding the weeds in your heart? Be very mindful of what you are watching. Be very careful with who you are listening to. This may include your drive to work and home. You may want to drive in silence or pray out loud. Silence and meditation may be a blessing. You may want to listen to worship music or a sermon. However, be careful not to allow defiling words into your ears because they go to your heart. What we watch and listen to has an impact as well. This would include the company that you keep. Be very close to your words. Negative talk will keep you in bondage. Be intentional about speaking God's word out loud.

Guard Your Heart

The world has encouraged the guarding of the heart. The goal is to avoid feelings being hurt in relationships. This is unavoidable. People are sinful and often fail to live up to expectations. Maybe the issue is not people. Is it possible that expectations are way too high? If you want to ensure that your heart is guarded, give your heart to the Lord instead. He is trustworthy and faithful. Once you have purged your heart and cleansed your heart, be careful not to allow the wrong desires back in. "Keep your heart with all vigilance, for from it flow the springs of life" (Proverb 4:23).

Once the Lord has led you to reorganize your heat and priorities, it is important to maintain it. Hopefully your heart will be more spiritual than carnal, like the one below.

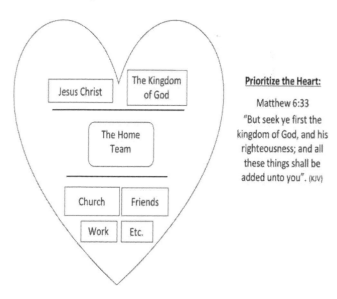

Jesus Christ

The Kingdom of God

The Home Team

Church   Friends

Work   Etc.

Prioritize the Heart:

Matthew 6:33
"But seek ye first the kingdom of God, and his righteousness; and all these things shall be added unto you". (KJV)

Figure 6. Prioritized Heart

Express Authentic Love

Husbands and Wives come into marriages with their individual desires, goals, and dreams. God intended for you to adopt the dreams that He has for you while forsaking your own. It is good to synchronize your goals to make sure that you and your spouse have the same expectations. This is going to require God's guidance, much patience and sacrifice too. You will have to sacrifice what you want individually to seek what your home team needs collectively. As you become one with your spouse, your desires, goals, and dreams will become one. Your individual goals will merge into one. The whole goal of marriage is to glorify God by working in harmony as a team.

Team Jewel
Your vision needs to synchronize with that of your spouse. Allow the unified vision of your home team to align with the plan that the Lord has for your team. Let Him provide the vision and submit to it.

The Bible talks about physical circumcision in the Old Testament. The New Testament talks about the necessity of circumcising the heart. God is making it clear that all people need a heart transplant. It's not that we don't have a heart currently. We have things that we desire, but they are inherently selfish. God promises that when we become believers in Jesus Christ, He will provide new desires of the heart. This is great news! The old desires of the heart must fade away.

> *And I will give you a new heart, and a new spirit I will put within you. And I will remove the heart of stone from your flesh and give you a heart of flesh (Ezekiel 36:26)*

Your relationship with Christ will have the strongest impact on your relationship with your spouse. Your spiritual condition in marriage is everything. Husbands will have a good heart toward their wives only when they learn to love Christ first. God teaches husbands what real love is and then they can demonstrate love to their wives fully. Spouses across the nation do not understand why they are unable to receive the love of their mate. This is difficult because love is not truly understood. God is love, and we must go to Him to learn true love. Going to church occasionally and reading the Bible occasionally will not adequately equip believers to love their spouses well. Some spouses want to love their mate but fail because they have a hardened heart. Some women truly desire to respect and submit to their husbands, but they can't because they need a new heart. Couples struggle to put their desires to the side and love God fully because they need a new heart. Your desires need to be sacrificed on the altar. Until that occurs, you will not fully know or experience what God has in store for your home team. When both you and your spouse glorify God by sacrificing your desires, your marriage will be unstoppable.

Pass the Love Test

Nobody likes to take tests. Tests are designed to be challenging. If students were allowed to design their exam, they would be very easy. That is exactly why a teacher is necessary. If the test is too easy, then learning and growth are unlikely. If tests are too difficult, they would be more harmful than helpful. Every student needs to be tested. Every student needs a teacher, and all great teams must be tested. The testing process is what pushes them to become great. A great test develops character, confidence and determination. Tests are a continuation of the learning process. Without being tested, few teams will ever become great.

Coaches set up pre-scheduled tests so that opponents will not blindside the team. The coach does so because he knows that his team will face tough opposition. The coach's assignment is to make sure that his team will be ready when that time comes. Pre-scheduled tests and scrimmages will attempt to mimic what the opponent will do. The main goal is preparation. If the team is fully prepared, then the likelihood of victory is greatly enhanced. Likewise, God will often test our faith and love for Him. Being tested by God is good and necessary for believers.

Testing is actually how I found my wife. Tasha and I were not close friends initially. We were associates who lived in different locations. I respected Tasha, and we talked very sparingly. Our relationship began to evolve when we had to face personal tests. One of the most difficult tests of all time was facing the loss of a loved one. Tasha's mother passed away after a terrible car accident. Her name was Selene Swazet Stokes. My grandmother, who helped raise me, passed away at the ripe age of 83. Her name was Loretta Australya Towns. This all occurred within a matter of months. We simply called each other and requested prayer. It was at that moment that Tasha and I went from being associates to prayer partners. Neither of us was romantically interested in the other, but we both needed a listening ear. We needed empathy. We needed someone that we could count on to go before God with intercession.

Prayer empowered us to weather the storms of death. I believe that Tasha became a stronger woman. Her faith grew as a result. I became a stronger man. I became more acquainted with Christ as a result. After the mourning, Tasha and I were no longer prayer partners. We had now become friends. It was the testing that exposed the friend that we had in each other. Without the testing, we would not have known the friend that we had in Jesus through prayer.

If you are rooted in Christ, testing will make you stronger. Testing will encourage you to bond with your spouse and to depend on the Lord. My prayer is that the trials of life will bring your home team together instead of separating you. God's plan is that these challenges will act like a glue that brings you together even in tough times. If handled properly, testing will help to fortify your marriage. Use your trials as a reason to persevere instead of an excuse to quit.

It is important to be reminded that God is the one that allows the testing to take place. Teachers rarely want to have their students fail. If you are going through a tough time right now, God has no intention of hurting you. He knows and understands your pain. He does not want you to fail the test. God only wants you and your spouse to have a closer relationship with him. He plans to use the storm to facilitate your growth. With God's help, your home team will be better prepared to weather storms.

The Promise Continues

When God reaffirmed His commitment in chapter 17, it was roughly 13 years after the grave mistake was made. Abram and Sarai may have given up. There is no recorded word from God in over a decade. Both of them are close to 100 years old, and they just committed a major infraction against God and His plan. Now, God has assured them that he has not forsaken them even though they had forsaken God. Sometimes when God is saying wait, it might feel like He is saying no.

He instead refuses to deviate from the original plan.

> *"And I will make my covenant between me and thee, and will multiply thee exceedingly. And Abram fell on his face: and God talked with him, saying, as for me, behold, my covenant is with thee, and thou shalt be a father of many nations" (Genesis 17:2-4)*

Beyond all of their faults, God kept His promise. Spouses will succeed when practicing this level of grace. God's love is proven by grace and mercy that he extends.

God had not given up on them. After a decade, God reaffirms His commitment by providing new names to both of them. Abram's name was changed to Abraham. Sarai's name was changed to Sarah. Abram means "exalted father," but Abraham means "father of a multitude." (Genesis 17:5) Sarai and Sarah both have the same root and meaning. Sarah was a "princess." They were shedding their old identity in order to identify with who God designed them to become.

It is clear Abram and Sarai are not worthy to be heirs of this promise and inheritance. However, neither are we worthy of receiving God's grace through Jesus Christ. Those who are dipped in the waters of baptism according to the covenant of Christ do not walk in perfection afterward. Neither would Abraham and Sarah walk in perfection after their covenant with God. As God refused to give up on the covenant with Abram, you should refuse to give up on your covenant with your spouse. Commit to authentic love by forgiving as Christ forgave you. Demonstrate to your spouse that they married a grace giver.

Promise not Forgotten

God approaches Abraham to remind him of His original promise over a decade ago. I could only imagine what their thoughts and feelings were after all of this time. After sixteen years, God approaches Abram yet again.

> *"When Abram was ninety-nine years old the Lord appeared to Abram and said to him, "I am God Almighty; [a] walk before me, and be blameless." (Genesis 17:1)*

No promise yet. Plenty of sin and confusion has occurred. However, God had not forgotten the promise that He made. Abraham is now 99 years old. God has promised Abraham in spite of all of the mistakes that he has made. God tells Abram to be blameless. It seems a little late for that right now. God still establishes a covenant with him to prove His unconditional love and His divine will.

Because of this relationship, Abraham becomes a new man. His name is changed. Is it possible that Abraham was uncapable of a better witness because he had yet to be in a covenant relationship with Him? Is it possible that Abraham had yet to receive the promise of God because he failed to commit to God through a covenant? They were missing the blessings of God because their hearts were after the blessings instead of the creator of those blessings. Their emotions were entangled in the promise. Before

God granted the blessing to Abraham and Sarah, He first wanted to give them the greatest gift, and that was a covenant relationship.

A Sealed Promise

The Covenant involved physical circumcision which was part of the Jewish culture and religious right. It was a foreshadowing of the covenant that He would establish with the people of God through Jesus Christ. It was prophesied by the prophets Ezekiel and Jeremiah (Jeremiah 24:7; Ezekiel 36:26), declaring that the new covenant would include the circumcision of the heart. God's people needed a sincere desire for Him instead of having a desire for what He could do for them. Heart circumcision was always God's intention. Listen to what God declared to His servant Moses. "Circumcise therefore the foreskin of your heart and be no more stiff-necked." (Deuteronomy 10:16). God was primarily concerned with their heart condition. The term stiff-necked refers to their inability and unwillingness to turn from their wicked ways. God wanted their heart.

The old stony heart would not allow them to practice repentance and true transformation. This became a consistent struggle. God's words to Moses proves that hearts still needed changing. "And the Lord their God will circumcise thine heart, and the heart of thy seed, to love the Lord thy God with all thine heart, and with all thy soul, that thou mayest live." (Deuteronomy 30:6) Abraham and Sarah would be unable to follow God until their heart condition changed.

God continues to make bold declarations. He first declares that He will establish the covenant with Abraham. From the very beginning, God has been initiating everything in regard to the Covenant. God initiated the conversation. God provided directions on what Abraham would do. God provided the promise. God delivered on all of these promises. God did everything that was done right in the covenant. This declares His consistent faithfulness to Abraham. It also exposes Abraham's lack of faithfulness to God. It is still hard to understand why God still chose a covenant with Abraham after his massive failures.

Marital relationships are no different. The covenant that you have with your spouse has nothing to do with your perfection. The covenant has everything to do with love and keeping the vow. Remember, that you and your spouse are in the same situation. You have both failed to uphold your end of the covenant with God. The Christian life is full of mistakes and sin. We are not even worthy to be in a covenant with God, but the perfect love of Jesus Christ made it all possible. As God has displayed love to you with no conditions, He wants you to display the same love to your spouse without conditions. Be intentional just as God was intentional with establishing a covenant of love with Abraham.

In the same passage, God declared that the covenant He established with Abraham was not temporary, but it was everlasting. (Genesis 17:17) There was nothing Abraham could do wrong to break the covenant. There was nothing Abraham could do right to earn the covenant either. Regardless of what Abraham did or did not do, God promised to establish a covenant that would be everlasting. God's goal was not to just establish a covenant with Abraham, but the promise was for his whole household and the generations that would come after him.

Always look at your marriage as an everlasting covenant. The vows say until death do us part. Maintain your marital covenant because of the promise that you made before God. Don't create harmful conditions within the covenant. As God has established an eternal covenant with you through Christ Jesus, He intends for you to maintain a covenant of love with your spouse. The everlasting covenant has nothing to do with emotions or romanticism. Those things are good but what God is presenting is His true love through His unconditional commitment. Serve and love your spouse regardless of how they treat you. In doing so, you will glorify God and bless them as a result.

When have you denied yourself in order to walk in obedience before God? Where can you grow in living and loving sacrificially? Please explain

_____

_____

_____

_____

_____

CHAPTER **7**

TEAM TALKS

*"The most important thing in communication
is to hear what isn't being said."*
—Peter F. Drucker

"In teamwork, silence isn't golden, it's deadly."
—Mark Sanborn

Drucker and Sandborn's statements present the necessity of good communication. Silence is on one extreme and talking too much on the other extreme. However, great communication demands a willingness to listen to others and to close our mouths. Great communication and conflict resolution are the signs of solid home teams. They are also signs of great corporations.

Some companies have the privilege of experiencing massive growth. That growth may lead to them going public and having their stocks sold. This is a great opportunity for companies to raise capital. It is also an opportunity for shareholders to invest in the company and yield a return. The Security Exchange Commission has put regulations in place to ensure the financial protection of consumers. Many years ago, an increase in consumer exploitation demonstrated a need for reform. Without the laws, financial sharks could take advantage of consumers. Some companies lack ethics and profit are king. Some ambitious executives are willing to do whatever it takes to gain market share. Selfishness in the form of greed will cause people to do unethical things.

One of these unethical practices is insider trading. High-level executives obtain critical information that would highly influence the financial decisions of other corporations and individual investors. The problem is that the information is not made public yet. That "insider" information is shared privately to only a small group of people before it becomes public. Insider trading is very sneaky and selfish. It seeks to help a few, while others are negatively impacted due to their lack of knowledge. Traders that are not in the know miss the opportunity to benefit from a pivotal swing in the market. This activity is against the law. Anyone that is found participating in insider trading will potentially face hefty fines and jail time.

Documentaries and movies have been produced to reenact these situations. Many of those high-level executives and companies profited large amounts off of the "insider" information they received. Others realized large losses as a result. With insider trading, the rich tend to get richer. In addition to that, the regular folk lose big. Information is selfishly shared with friends when it often should be kept private.

Think about it, shouldn't the "insider" information of your home team be kept private also? Your home team needs communication, but It is wise to be selective on what you communicate and who you are communicating with. Few are selective of who they communicate with while single. Singleness is a time full of freedom. However, when couples get married, things should begin to change. There is a larger need to consider how your communication will impact your spouse. When couples get married, everything changes. The information we receive, and share has the potential to hurt other people. The hidden information of the heart can be detrimental as well.

Keep it in the Locker Room

The locker room is a place of great significance for a sports team. Several unique things occur in the locker room. The locker room is a place where teammates get undressed, so it is a place of transparency. In the locker room, athletes deal with their injuries, so it is a place of vulnerability. The locker room is a place of relaxation, so it is a place of peace. The locker room is where teammates shower and get cleaned up before going out in public. It is a place where you can look in the mirror with privacy. The locker room may involve a conversation about specific strategies and game plans for the team. The locker room will probably include passionate discussions. It is a place where inside information should be kept private.

There will be difficult seasons of your life that will include challenges. There is nothing like coming home to your home team. Home is where the heart is. Home should be a place of safe shelter. It should be a haven full of encouragement. You may come home bruised and battered from the world. However, the home should be a place where your wounds can be consoled. Support from your home team will allow you to endure the struggles of life. However, certain discussions need to be kept between your spouse and God.

Are you guarding heated discussions and debates in the locker room? If you have an accountability partner, is God the first person that you speak to? If your spouse publicly troubles you, it is best to hold your peace. Wait until it can be discussed behind the closed doors of the locker room. If possible, do not have heated discussions in public and the presence of others.

The locker room is an intimate place where you and your spouse can discuss important matters of the team. Your locker room may be the bedroom. It might be the living room while the kids are at school. It might be anywhere in the privacy of your home. Remember, even though no one else is physically present, God is also in your midst. In your marital conversation, practice patience as well as self-control. Whenever you have an opportunity to dialogue with your spouse, make sure that you do these things:

Ask: Remember that it is important to ask first because you do not want to assume anything. Assuming will make you look silly, and it will eventually hurt your spouse because your assumptions may not be accurate. Being presumptuous tends to create division and hurt feelings. Trust is very important to your spouse. Assuming presents that you lack trust in them. Ask questions first and draw conclusions later. Be patient; God will eventually reveal the truth in love.

Give Benefit of the Doubt: You and I are going to do things or say things that will hurt our spouses. This is often not the intent. However, it helps when you realize that your spouse did so unintentionally. Regardless of what happened, these discussions are important to let your spouse know that you trust them and that you know that they would not hurt you intentionally. Words like this may be helpful: I know that you did not mean to, but what you did really hurt my feelings. What were your true intentions? Or maybe something like this: You probably did not even notice but you left the television on again, and I was upset. Wouldn't you prefer to receive benefit of doubt from your spouse? When your spouse's intentions are good, happily grant grace to them.

Be Transparent: It is important to let your teammate know your true feelings. Share these feelings with temperance and consideration. Remember that God made you and your spouse differently, so you will naturally receive things differently. If truth is not communicated openly, your teammate will never see your perspective. True understanding requires considering your spouse's viewpoint. Practice transparency with God first. If you tend to hide things from the Lord, it is likely that you will do the same with your spouse. Be honest with yourself and tell the whole truth to God. You might as well because He already knows everything (Ps 147:5). Coming clean with yourself and God will prepare you to do the same with your spouse. You have to practice this because it won't just happen on its own. Transparency is vital, and it builds trust.

Reconcile and resolve: Seek ways to avoid the same issues in the future. The beauty of when you come out of the locker room is that no one knows about the struggle, the disagreements or the tension. The goal is to prevent a recurrence in the future and to get on one accord. It is important for you to remain intentional and strategic about communicating with each other. This is an example of working together as a team. When spouses don't trust each other, they reinforce selfish behaviors. Be sure to maintain respect beyond all circumstances.

> *Men need to feel respected during conflict more than they need to feel loved. This does not mean men do not need love. (Eggerichs 58)*

Throughout the process, respect will aid reconciliation. Without mutual respect, your home team will be full of tension. Disrespectful teams do not win much. When your spouse wins, so do you. When championship teams win, everybody gets a ring. Everyone on the team is a champion and is acknowledged as a contributor to the team's success. I pray that you will begin to see your spouse as a blessed asset to the home team. Let's face it, it is much better to work together than live in tension.

Follow the Rules of Engagement

Please avoid having these discussions around your children. Beyond that, make sure that you are not speaking loud enough for your children to hear the conversation from the other room. It is none of their business. This is between you, your spouse and God. Only teammates are allowed in the locker room. Children are hurt by seeing mommy and daddy in disagreement. It's good for children to realize that mommy and daddy are different and see things differently. They need to know that mommy and daddy will eventually come to an agreement and stand together as such. Allow your children to know that you care more about their heart more than winning a silly argument with your spouse. What is truly sad is that these same selfish behaviors are often emulated by children who learn from their parents. Begin to consider the big picture.

For that reason, it is important to be selective on whom you may share information with. I recommend that you do not share any information about your marriage or spouse with anyone. You may want to talk to an elder at your church if needed. The goal is to identify someone more spiritually mature than you are. We all need someone to challenge us to handle things appropriately. Only share these things with someone you are sure will keep them confidential. Share with prayerful people. Avoid people that will agree with everything that you do or say. You want someone that is going to tell you that you are wrong, point you to the Scripture and pray for you in the process. It is good for every spouse to have at least one person like this. Take an assessment of your circle of accountability. Your circle is probably more impactful than you might realize.

Avoid Loose Talk

The phrase "loose lips sinks ships" is an American English idiom that became popular during World War II. What the idiom is trying to make clear is that you have to be careful with unguarded talk. The phrase was a warning against conversation that can be very detrimental to the American team. It's hard to imagine how conversation can lead to death. When ships sink, people die. However, ships don't sink on their own. During war, ships and submarines may face torpedoes. Often, the enemy is unable to know where to send the torpedoes unless they have insider information. Think about it, the only way that inside information can reach the enemy is if someone on the home team has unguarded talks and speaks loosely. I am not saying that the people around you are your enemies. What I am saying is that your adversary, the devil, utilizes unsaved and immature people to sow words of discord that can ultimately hurt your marriage.

Unguarded talk comes from unguarded hearts. If your mind roams with imaginations that are unguarded, that will also impact your speech. As a result, you will speak in an unguarded way. It is not what goes in that defiles a man, but it's what comes out. To watch your tongue, you must first watch your heart.

Life is fluid; very seldom is it stable. The environment around us consistently changes. Conditions become altered. The seasons are always changing. That is why they are called seasons. We cannot control the weather. If you pay attention to the changes, you can better equip yourself to weather storms. You should begin to expect changes because the adventurous walk with Jesus Christ is full of fluidity.

Weather the Storms

Because your marriage was blessed yesterday does not ensure that you will experience harmony in future seasons. Couples have to be intentional about maintaining harmony and positive momentum in their marriage. The Bible presents several principles that will ensure success no matter what challenges they face. I can easily name a few. Obedience to God is important. Prayerfulness is extremely important. Humility is a necessity. Being considerate of your partner is extremely important, and surely, communication is key. This is just to name a few. Whenever couples become complacent, they lose spiritual momentum.

As strange as it may sound, sports teams go through some of the same challenges as your home team. Consider this, it is possible to be complacent with your previous victories. Teams may begin to underestimate their opponent because they dominated for most of the game. Therefore, they go into the halftime not being very aware or cognitively sharp. Pride has crept in. They feel like they have all that it takes to destroy their opponent and eventually fall in defeat because of being overconfident.

Likewise, Satan has an assignment to steal, kill and destroy families (John 10:10). The devil has been very successful doing that throughout the years. In your home team, there will be a season where things are going extremely well. When complacency develops, it goes right into the enemy's plan. When you relax, that is when the enemy is known to attack. Stay diligent in your devotion to the Lord and you will always be ready to stand.

> *Therefore, my beloved brothers, be steadfast, immovable, always abounding in the work of the Lord, knowing that in the Lord your labor is not in vain (1 Corinthians 15:58).*

Being immovable is contingent on your diligence in abounding in the work of the Lord. Faithful laboring for the Lord will act as a strong defense against the enemy's strategy against your home team.

It is impossible to have a utopian marriage and live in a vacuum where problems no longer exist. We live in a fallen society that is populated with fallen people. People are made in God's image, but we consistently make bad choices. The Bible identifies these poor choices as sin. Without God's grace and a changed heart, it is not possible to have good character. Even Christians struggle to have a renewed heart and a transformed mind. As long as we live in this world, problems will exist.

What? You thought I was going to give you advice on how to get rid of your problems? I am sorry to disappoint you. Remember that God never promised to get rid of our problems. What He did promise is that He would never leave nor forsake us, which means that He will give us the strength and guidance to navigate through our problems. If God brings you to it, He is faithful and able to bring you through it. God's plan is not to remove our problems. He does not want couples to retreat in fear. God intends for couples to face these challenges together with faith.

Unfortunately, many families face tribulations in their marriage and begin to ponder separation and divorce. If you have an enemy in the house, then make them into an ally. Teammates often struggle to see eye-to-eye, but the team will be much better when they see each other as an asset. It is essential for you and your spouse to work together as a team because you won't be able to do so in isolation. The locker room is about changing and making adjustments! The locker room is about encouraging your teammate! It is a time to identify mistakes with love and honesty. It is a time of rest and relaxation. Use the locker room to listen to your heavenly coach. Find spiritual hydration for your parched soul. The locker room is about taking a proactive pause to get your home team together. Emerge from your private space ready to follow Christ and tackle the world...together.

Team Jewel

Maintain your hope and joy in all situations. Optimism is contagious. Find your joy in your faithful Father and not in the unstable world.

It is a waste of energy to worry about what is happening to the home team. Worry will produce anxiety. Anxiety will produce fatigue. The home team must come to this conclusion: if we follow our game plan and live according to God's divine design, then we will be able to weather any storm that comes our way. Activate your faith and God to increase it. (Luke 17:5)

Rest in His Strength

God wants to prove that He is trustworthy and safer, but He won't force you to give Him the opportunity. If you are going through a storm and a difficult season right now, I encourage you to stop relying on your strength!

Put it all in the Lord's hands instead. Scripture says come unto me all that are heavy laden and burdened down and I will give you rest, (Matthew 11:28-29). In this passage, God is giving an invitation for us to receive His rest. A lot of people sleep at night but still never get any rest. It is possible to close your eyes for a full 8 hours straight and not actually be resting. When we have worry and anxiety, our body shuts down, but our mind continues to wrestle with certain matters.

A lot of anxiety sets in when you have no idea which way to go. Good teams rely on the consultation of their coach. They know that he is going to put them in a position to win. Through prayer, you can tap into God's consultation and receive the game plan that He has for your life. It is possible to be in the midst of a very difficult season of your life but still be at total peace. This is only obtained when you put your cares in the Master's hands. This is only obtained when you have a consultation with your heavenly coach.

There is also an eternal rest for your soul. Our bodies will decay and eventually return to the dust from which it came (Ecclesiastes 3:20; 12:7). However, your spirit shall live forever. God has given an invitation to choose Him by faith. He has promised us that our souls will have eternal rest with Him in heaven. This will provide peace in the current moment knowing that no matter what happens today or tomorrow, you shall win in the end. If you are born again, you are on the winning team and have the all-time winningest coach on the sidelines. Be encouraged because winning is now in your DNA.

Bad weather may come in the form of job loss. This could be after the loss of a loved one. This could be in in form of making a very important decision concerning my child. It can be regarding my spouse's Health. There are seasons that will require an emergency timeout. Your knowledge is finite; this is a perfect time to have a peaceful talk with the Lord. Whenever coaches see their team struggling or failing to execute, the coach signals a timeout to talk it over with his team. The goal is to get the home team back on track and back on the path to winning. All teams should take timeouts to get back on track.

Share at the Table

Many years ago, family life was centered at home. One of the most intricate parts of family life was dinner time. This was a time when children would share what happened in school; fathers would talk about what happened at their job; wives would share thoughts. The family sits down together. The family would sit, talk and eat together.

Team Jewel
A family that sits, eats and has devotion together should stay together.

Imagine what our culture would be like today if families still took time out to just eat together and talk to each other. The family should communicate together regularly. It does not have to be a special occasion, but it is a tradition that strengthens the family.

Over the years, tradition has gotten a bad name in general. I love to get rid of old things. Sometimes, old stuff is outdated and needs to be replaced. However, America has lost an understanding of what community is and has replaced it with electronic devices and television. Home teams across the nation have produced young adults with weak communication skills. Spouses struggle to build bonds with their mates. As a result, the modern family has produced a working family that is too busy to sit down together, eat, and talk.

Family time has been replaced by sports. Children have adopted the busy culture of their parents and spend all year worshipping sports achievements. Some achieve accolades, but many lose love for God as a result. Fathers are ruled by the allure of climbing the corporate ladder and providing for their families. Money has become more important than spending time with the home team. Some families have even replaced Sunday devotion with the worship of sports, leisures, and other idols.

Please don't misunderstand what I'm saying. I played three sports in high school and two in college. Sports are a great tool for learning life lessons. However, things get out of balance when sports become an idol. Family time is the perfect opportunity to testify of God's goodness and point your home team to the Lord. Listen to the Hughes Family explain their family devotion:

> *"Typically, our worship at the table has included Scripture, prayers and a hymn."* (Hughes 51)

At the end of the day, your family devotion will have a much greater impact than worshipping the glory of athletics. Your devotion to the Lord will have a generational and eternal impact. Please do not allow your home team to develop a habit of idol worship because it is very destructive.

The appeal of competitive sports is strong from many American families. Merging the two is ideal through a ministry like Fellowship of Christian Athletes. If your home team is struggling with balancing these things, please search for a local FCA chapter in your city. The ministry has helped youth avoid idolatry by celebrating Jesus while competing. My family has been blessed through the ministry and I encourage any family involved in amateur sports to get involved. Check out their website: www.fca.org

---

Team Jewel
Worship God and nothing else. Guard your family against everything. Spend time with God together.

Talk When It Is Inconvenient

Over the years Tasha and I had a major challenge when we went from a two-person household to a five-person household immediately. Our daughter was being born, and we inherited two teenagers (Tasha's young brothers) because the boys' father passed away abruptly. This required Tasha to stay home and take care of our newborn daughter while assisting the new teenage additions to the family. This was the busiest time of my life. I was juggling work, a business and seminary. With God's grace, we made it through. Sometimes, too many "good" things can have a negative impact. It is important to emphasize the fact that idols can arise from good desires as well as wicked ones. "It is often not what we want that is the problem, but that we want it too much." (Sande 104). Our efforts were based on a healthy desire to be a blessing. It was important for us to guard our hearts against allowing good things to be our primary focus and not the Lord.

Families have to fight against busyness to maintain the most important things. During that season, my home team did not necessarily eat at the dinner table every night. We had to make necessary adjustments in order to maintain our relationships. The most important thing to do is refuse to be an idol worshipper. Do not allow anything to become more important than the Lord in your home. If your occupation, hobbies, sports or anything interfere with your heavenly relationship, I will encourage you to make adjustments immediately. All idols will attack your relationship with God and your spouse.

The dinner table exists to help protect you against these distractions. It calls you from the busy routines of life to enjoy a refreshing meal and conversation with those who are the closest. It gives you an opportunity to listen to each other and express love to one another by sharing your time with them. Once you begin to make family devotions and conversation a priority, relationships within your home team will be stronger.

Team Jewel
Make dinner time important in your home. Require that electronic devices are removed. Turn off the television. Become invested in communicating with your family without distractions.

Table Traditions

The table is supposed to be a place of joy and laughter. The table is where we pray for God's grace upon each other. The table can be a place to testify about God's goodness. In times past, the table was a place of worship.

When I was young, I was raised by my mother who was a single parent. While she was at work, I spent a lot of time with her parents and her aunt. They all lived in the same house and a small community called Alpha Gardens. It was a close-knit community. I was born right around the time that my grandfather retired. I was always involved in athletics, and I loved to be outside. At this time, kids did not spend much time with video games. We used television to entertain ourselves when we couldn't go outside. One of the worst punishments a kid could ever get would be a restriction from enjoying the outdoors.

There were two simple rules that my grandparents had for me. The first rule was when you come in from school, complete your homework immediately. The other rule was that supper is at 5:30. No matter what I was doing, I had to come in and eat with the rest of the family. The elders didn't care how much fun we were having outside. It didn't matter if we were in the middle of a highly contested basketball game. The only thing that mattered was that supper was a priority for my elders. I did not want to get in hot water, so I obeyed. At the dinner table we laughed, talked and prayed. I shall never forget the time that we spent.

Today I am extremely thankful that my grandparents did not bend on that rule. All three of those elders passed away well over a decade ago. My life has been enriched by the amount of wisdom that I obtained during those weekday dinners at the table. It has made me a better man, and I had great friendships with all three of them because of the intimate time that we spent together. In my life, these moments were priceless! The same would be true for your home team. Invest your time and focus where it counts.

Use Innovation to Counter Being B-U-S-Y

Be careful with busyness. A common acronym for busy is: Buried Under Satan's Yoke. I believe that the enemy has a scheme of keeping believers busy, so they do not give God the attention and worship that He deserves.

During these busy seasons, my wife and I had to make some adjustments, and I will encourage you to do the same. If the evening time was difficult for her and I to get together, we would use the mornings. If the mornings were too difficult, then we would use the weekends. The point is that we made sure that we scheduled that time because it was extremely important to us.

My wife is a coffee connoisseur. I never even drank coffee before I got married. It didn't taste that great, and it didn't keep me awake. That is because I never had a cup that Tasha prepared before. Today, I can say that I might drink two cups a week. The point is that Tasha loves coffee. During the week of our busy season, we would wait until Natalie was in school and we would stop for a moment and have a cup of coffee together at the table. It was a time for us to talk about what was going on. It was a time for us to pray together. It was also a time to have a short devotion. It was always refreshing for our souls to get together in a quiet setting at home and just talk and pray. If you are in a busy season right now, don't be discouraged. You may have to incorporate ingenuity. The point is that you make adjustments to make sure that you get together. Intentionality is important. God understands that you're busy, but He does not want you to give it up so easily. I'm sure that if you make that a priority, He will help you make it a reality.

Strange Visitors

Early in the passage, Abraham is met by two guests. It may not have been uncommon for guests to visit them. However, Abraham did not just greet them as regular men. He displayed a greater amount of respect and hospitality. Based on his response, these were not ordinary men. Not only did Abraham rush to great them, but he also and worshipped.

> *"And he lift up his eyes and looked, and, lo, three men stood by him: and when he saw them, he ran to meet them from the tent door, and bowed himself toward the ground, and said, My Lord, if now I have found favor in thy sight, pass not away, I pray thee, from thy servant:"* (Genesis 18:2-3)

The men were messengers from the Lord. Abraham knew that he was in the presence of God by entertaining God's messengers. These messengers came to deliver a message to his household. Abraham worked tirelessly to accommodate them. Hospitality was an important aspect of Jewish culture. However, worship is reserved for God alone. Not even angels should be worshipped. Listen to what the angel told John when he tried to worship him,

> *"Then I fell down at his feet to worship him, but he said to me, "You must not do that! I am a fellow servant with you and your brothers who hold to the testimony of Jesus."* (Revelation 19:10) *John then made the same mistake and he received the same rebuke, but he said to me, "You must not do that! I am a fellow servant with you and your brothers the prophets, and with those who keep the words of this book. Worship God."* (Revelation 22:9)

Even the angel was very adamant that worship is reserved for God alone!

The messengers were on a divine mission. They came to reaffirm them of God's original promise. The men declared unto Abram that his wife, Sarah was still going to bear a son. God had not forgotten them. I am pretty sure that Abraham and Sarah had major concerns and considered giving up. It has been decades of waiting. Their faith in the promise had become weary and weak. Sarah was so old. The promise came when she was around 65. She has been waiting around for 25 years. Her hormones had changed. She had probably endured menopause. The possibility of her conceiving was laughable to her. It is not uncommon for God to give you a mission or a promise that seems impossible. Listen to the question submitted to Sarah.

> *Is anything too hard for the LORD? At the time appointed I will return unto thee, according to the time of life, and Sarah shall have a son. (Genesis 18:14)*

Communication between husband and wife can sometimes sound or seem difficult because the perspective of the husband and wife are different. Abraham did not question what the men had said. He seemed to receive it wholeheartedly. The same could not be said about his wife, Sarah.

Abraham had a conversation with the messengers first. Talking to God's heavenly messengers was symbolic of the ongoing conversation with God. Notice that Abram had a conversation with heaven before conversing with anyone else, even his wife. This is critical. As a leader, it is critical that you possess a clear vision. This requires knowing where to go, what to do and when. The only person that has this foresight is God. The only way that we can have a vision for the future is to consult with He who knows all things. Abraham did well to make communication with God primary. This was surely a winning principle for his family.

Abraham is trying to believe God, even though circumstances express the contrary. In a democratic state of America, rights are supreme. Rights are sometimes worshipped more than God is. That is true for some now but what about back then? Let's consider Sarah's situation a little bit. What if Sarah did not want to give birth to Isaac? Perhaps she wanted a son, years ago but now has different feelings. Does she have the right to tell God no? The answer is yes. God has granted them liberty to walk in obedience. Sarah may have felt that she was not included in the plans. The disobedience in Sarah's heart was both towards God and her husband. She was led by her emotions instead of God, and it weighed heavily on her faith. Her emotions were contrary to God's will.

> *Now Abraham and Sarah were old and well stricken in age: and it ceased to be with Sarah after the manner of women. Therefore, Sarah laughed within herself, saying, after I am waxed old shall I have pleasure, my Lord being old also? (Genesis 18:11-12)*

Sarah laughed within herself because she was in disbelief of what she had heard. These were her authentic feelings and emotions. Emotions are real and cannot be ignored. Often, emotions antagonize the will of God. Sarah had every right to feel the way she felt. The passage makes it very clear that Sarah had checked out. Her patience had eroded over the years. Her heart and thoughts were ungodly. God's ways and thoughts are so much higher than ours (Isaiah 55:8-9). It is wise to follow God's ways even when they make little sense.

Sarah did what you should not do. When her true feelings were exposed, she tried to cover it up. Sarah quickly conjured up a lie. Sarah did laugh internally, and she knew within her heart she was lying. What is very important in this process is that husbands and wives be very transparent with their emotions. It is wise to first be transparent with the Lord. Through prayer, let God know how you feel. Tell Him how you truly feel. Trust me, God can take it. He already knows how you feel but he wants you to share these intimate things with Him willingly. God wants you to also share with your spouse. There's no need to hide with God or our spouse. Sharing produces a deeper intimacy and a closer relationship. It is very likely that Sarah has had these strong emotions bottled up for the past decade. She needed to face those feelings through a conversation with her husband and the Lord.

This was a huge deal for Sarah because bearing children had a strong connection to her value and worth of a woman. God promised her that she would have a child and all nations would be blessed through them. She was going to bear the seed of Abraham. Many women would sign up to be in her position. However, at this point, the down payment for her promise was her faith, and at this particular time, she was a little low in the faith department.

God was well aware of Sarah's faithlessness and the strong emotions that she felt. I truly feel that God did not draw near only to have a conversation with Abraham. After much time had passed, God sent messengers to encourage them both to hold on because the promise was almost there. The Lord was sending a messenger of encouragement to a discouraged couple, in order to restore hope. However, they needed to get on the same page. They needed to become one again and walk in agreement; this required an intimate conversation between the spouses and their heavenly coach.

Sarah needed Abraham to be more aware. God was not only using him to be the father of many nations. God had called Abraham to be a good husband and leader to Sarah first. Sarah was obviously in spiritual pain and anguish. The passage does not say much about Abraham's interaction with his wife. Husbands are not called to provide and protect only. God has also called husbands to nurture their wives spiritually. Paul gives this charge:

> *Husbands, love your wives, as Christ loved the church and gave himself up for her that he might sanctify her, having cleansed her by the washing of water with the word. (Ephesians 5:25-26)*

God has called for watchful soul care to begin at home. Husbands are called to lead their wives in the Word. Likewise, parents are called to make sure their children know the Lord. In difficult times like this, spouses need to become the biggest encouragers of their home team. When life weighs you down, remember that God understands. Your breakthrough will come from intimacy and transparency with the Lord and your spouse. This begins with real communication.

Do you feel that you and your spouse consistently experience true reconciliation after disagreements?

_____
_____
_____
_____
_____

Is communication with your spouse enjoyable and transparent? Please explain.

_____
_____
_____
_____
_____

CHAPTER **8**

HONEST REFLECTION

"Mistakes are always forgivable
if one has the courage to admit them."
—Bruce Lee

Anyone who knows of Bruce Lee's career, would probably think that he was not acquainted with mistakes. He was arguably the greatest martial artist of all time but surely committed mistakes during his life. Honesty and transparency are needed for home teams to thrive. Likewise, Ford Motor Company made mistakes over the years but has used them as a growth opportunity.

Over the years I've owned a couple of cars made by Ford Motor Company. The first car that I ever owned was a Ford. As I became an adult, I realized that Ford's reputation was pretty bad. Ford was not valued as a company that had produced quality products. I don't think that all of their products were bad, but they had some vehicles that hurt the brand. Some customers checked out and refused to buy another Ford vehicle. I remember watching a documentary while in business school at the University of Louisville. It explained some of the innovative changes that Ford was making under the leadership of their new president.

The first major change was in leadership. Alan Mullally took over at the helm. He already had a plan to implement positive change. Alan identified several barriers that needed to be removed for Ford to gain more respect. At the time, they were losing about 17 billion dollars annually. Mullally stated that within the company, there was a lot of fear of what the future held. He said the vision was weak and the strategies to implement that vision were weak as well. He acknowledged that the product was just not up to par. As a result, employees began to leave the company and customers began to jump ship as well. Mullally still was confident. He stated that throughout their long history, they always had great people in the organization. He believed this to be their greatest asset and the main reason for organizational optimism.

One of the adjustments that he made was to cast a compelling vision. He felt that vision was critical to enhancing morale with current employees. The vivid vision would infuse faith and remove fear. A voice was given to every one of the department heads. Their new leader wisely aligned the current vision with the original vision of Henry Ford. Henry Ford desired to open the highway to every American family. Luxury brands and models for wealthy customers were sold. They began to focus on creating vehicles that would be affordable for all Americans. Each perspective was now relevant.

The result was a great success. Ford gained a lot of market share during those years. Ford recaptured respect in the automobile industry and the marketplace. The trust of the consumer skyrocketed as well. All of these changes were big and challenging. These changes required patience and time. Ford owned the issues. The company culture progressed and the rest was history.

What you can learn from this is that change is required for growth. Internal transformation must occur before external growth. Honest assessments are great. Planning is extremely important, but action is equally important. Without action, plans die quickly. Furthermore, actions without plans are erratic. It is action that brings the vision to life. However, planning will add focus to your energy. After much time is spent crafting and revising a plan, your home team must focus on applying biblical principles to your lives. Honest assessment and action led to the resurgence of Ford. Likewise, godly reflection and a rededication to Christian values will lead to the revival of your home team.

God has designed for couples to both plan and to implement change. Marriage is meant to be a sanctifying process, but society has promoted worldly ideals. Ridiculous expectations have been the result. Engaged couples expect a dream spouse. Their flaws are hidden. The truth is that new husbands and wives have much learning and growing to do. This will require honest reflection. True growth is sparked by intentionally making changes. At the end of the day, home teams must be willing to change those things in order to grow and be more like Christ.

Review Mistakes

In every sport, coaches have their athletes watch game film. Not all athletes are excited about watching film. That is because very few people like to look at themselves in the mirror and review the imperfections they possess. Great coaches are experts at breaking down film. They understand the game so well that they see almost everything. Some coaches could spend hours looking at the different nuances of the game, while searching for new insight. The best coaches have forgotten more about the game than most will ever know. One of the coach's responsibilities is to help their athletes improve. Watching the film is a very important part of the improvement process. Athletes become uncomfortable because not only are their mistakes exposed, but they are revealed in front of their peers. Humility is often the result.

Your spouse can see what you can't. It is important for both of you to share what you see with love. God will grant discernment to you and your spouse. It is much better to receive honesty in private than to be exposed in public. It is probably easy to see these things in your spouse than to receive it from them. Rely on the Holy Spirit to reveal sin in your life through the Word as well. The process began with a simple question. Ask God to reveal sin in your life. Meditate on the Word and allow your heart to be searched. (Psalm 139:23).

Own Your Mistakes

It is in human nature to offer excuses for our mistakes. Trying to justify lousy decisions only makes things worse. The best thing to do is to take ownership and make a vow to improve. Once you are aware of your mistakes, it is not helpful to create excuses for them. Be honest with yourself and understand that at your best, you will still live a life of mistakes. The goal is to learn from them and avoiding repeating the same ones. The key to a changed life is a relationship with Jesus. Look at what Dr. Willie Richardson says.

> *"When people don't have salvation in Jesus Christ, they lead godless lives controlled by a sinful nature." (Richardson 18)*

Jesus Christ is the only answer to move from your sinful nature to a sanctified life. It is important to depend on the work of Christ and not your own.

If you feel like you have not contributed to a situation within the home team, take ownership anyway. It is likely that you somehow contributed to the issue or failed to contribute to the solution. Even if the blame is minimal, there might have been something that you could have done to help. Self-reflection will allow you to notice various opportunities to contribute to the health of the home team.

Offering an apology is very important. Be specific and genuine. Consider something like this: "I am so sorry that I hurt your feelings." "I failed to consider how that would impact you." Take your time with apologies. Communicate it with gentleness. Listen to Solomon's wisdom here, "a soft answer turns away wrath, but a harsh word stirs up anger." (Proverbs 15:1) Without self-reflection, the person will not know what they did to contribute to the issue.

That often means that it will probably resurface in the future. Apologies are great, but they must be specific, genuine and gentle.

If someone has reached repentance and have moved past an apology, the following actions will prove it. It is hard to sometimes apologize to others. Do your children ever struggle with apologizing? It even hurts them to realize that they are wrong. It is also good for you to realize how your wrongs have hurt others. It's good to look past your pain and see the hurt of others. Verbally apologizing is not nearly as helpful as taking action to make corrections. Everyone develops habits; some of them are good, and others are bad. However, change is requires being intentional and deliberate about moving in the right direction. That move will have to be according to God's word.

Grow From Your Mistakes

Throughout his life, Abraham had struggled to follow God. However, he had been chosen to be a recipient of God's promise. God established a covenant with Abraham and used him to be the father of many nations. His name will be forever etched in the Christian canon as one of the most important biblical characters. First, Abraham needed endurance for the journey. God had been maturing him over the years. God never told him when the promise would come, but it would have to be soon because he was old as dirt. It seemed as if God's promise would never come. Age was not the real issue. Abraham's real problem was his faith.

Think about it; Abraham's lack of faith caused him to do some very foolish things. Trusting God often looks silly. Abraham had to get up and leave the familiar surroundings of his family. He had to go to a place before knowing where it was. Abraham at this point had developed the skill of stepping out on faith. However, Abraham had not yet developed the ability to stay out on faith.

Abraham's fear was causing him to act out of emotion instead of obedience. When Abraham first started his adventure, he was failing in the faith category. He convinced his wife to lie and say that she was his sister. His fear made him paranoid. He was worried about danger when God had already ensured their safety. Abraham was really looking out for himself. There is no love in selfishness. He put his wife in danger so that he could be safe. Fear is the total antithesis of faith. Fear and faith are archnemeses and are in constant opposition within our hearts. Now does this sound like the great father Abraham who would become a role model of faithfulness? God had the plan to mature Abraham's faith so that he would be ready to receive the promise.

Everything is done in God's perfect timing and according to His perfect will. God will not provide promises and blessings before you can handle them. Abraham and Sarah questioned God, but He was not the problem. The problem resided in Abraham and Sarah. Premature blessings and elevations are catastrophic. As your home teams puts its trust in the Lord, understand that this means putting God's plan, method and timing all in His perfect hands.

Abraham was yet to learn from his previous mistakes. Yes, he wanted the promise, but he kept committing the same sins.

> *"And Abraham journeyed from thence toward the south country, and dwelled between Ka'desh and Shur, and sojourned in Ge'rar. And Abraham said of Sarah his wife, she is my sister: Abimelech king of Ge'rar sent, and took Sarah. But God came to Abimelech in a dream by night, and said to him, Behold, thou art a dead man, for the woman which thou hast taken; for she is a man's wife". (Genesis 20:1-3)*

Abraham is full of fear and lying to save himself again. Abraham again and puts his wife in danger. Abraham has yet to put his full faith and trust in God. This seemed to put the promise of God in jeopardy. God knows that if Abimelech takes Abraham's wife, then she can become pregnant with someone else's child. Abraham had already impregnated someone outside of the union. The great news is that their sinfulness was not as big as God's sovereignty. He stepped in to make sure that didn't happen. Humanity has a habit of sowing confusion, but God often steps in to save people from themselves.

God visits Abimelech in a dream and advised him not to take Sarah. Death would have been the result. Abimelech expressed his ignorance of the situation. It seemed that Abimelech had more faith in the promise of God than God's chosen man, Abraham. Abraham put Sarah in a difficult situation. He had also put Abimelech in danger as well.

Abimelech woke from his dream and told his servants about what happened. As a result, the men were afraid of the danger that they had been put in. Abimelech then approached Abraham to ask why he would lie. Abraham had no idea how bad he this made him look, God's leader, lying for no reason. Abraham's response is important.

> *What sawest thou, that thou hast done this thing? And Abraham said, because I thought, surely the fear of God is not in this place; and they will slay me for my wife's sake. (Genesis 20:10-11)*

Abraham ultimately gave an excuse that was based on his assumptions and had nothing to do with truth. He clearly explained that he was afraid. Abraham was still trying to learn how to trust God. This exposes the fact that Abraham was focused on saving himself and no one else. He was more interested in his thoughts than the promise of God. The fear of God not being there was irrelevant. It had everything to do with Abraham's concern for protection. Remember that God had worked out all of the details before He called him to the journey. He already had those things worked out. Your home team is surely no different. God knows where He is leading your family and He already has determined how you will get there.

Team Jewel
If you are going to trust God for provisions, you must trust Him also for His protection.

Abraham then blessed Abimelech by praying for him and asking for God's mercy upon him. This was what the Lord promised. God displayed His grace by putting it on Abimelech's heart to give resources to Abraham after his major blunder. When it seems like God should have punished Abraham, He gave him much grace and mercy instead. Abraham left with more resources than he came with. God's covenant was still intact. His promise seemed so far away but His promise was on the way.

Keep Believing

Abram started as a regular guy. He was following in his family's footsteps. He lived in the same region, around the same people, doing pretty much the same things. God abruptly interrupted all of the comfortability of Abram to set him on course to complete a godly mission.

Beyond that, the journey was full of adventure and promise. Within the decades of pursuing God's promise, Abram and Sarai allowed their sinful nature to surface. Their lives were plagued with lies, confusion, selfishness, tears, and fear. They did not seem like the right couple to be used to glorify God, but no matter how bad things got, God still decided to use them.

Strange as it may seem, the end of the story was much better than the beginning. Eventually, Abram became Abraham and a man full of faith. Sarai eventually matured and became Sarah. She conceived at a very old age and gave birth to Isaac, which was the seed that was promised by God. It took nearly 25 years for her to receive what God had promised.

All of this took place centuries before the birth of Christ, and the Messiah was born from the same bloodline. Faith was surely their

Achilles heel. The good news is that eventually, in the book of Hebrews, both Abraham and Sarah were praised for the faith that they eventually had in God. Neither was truly faithful, but they realized that God was.

> *By faith, Abraham obeyed when he was called to go out to a place that he was to receive as an inheritance. And he went out, not knowing where he was going (Hebrews 11:8)*

> *By faith, Sarah herself received power to conceive, even when she was past the age since she considered Him faithful who had promised. (Hebrews 11:11)*

God never said that Abraham or Sarah were righteous. Instead, He said that they had faith and it was counted to them as righteousness.

> *Therefore, from one man, and him as good as dead, were born descendants as many as the stars of heaven and as many as the innumerable grains of sand by the seashore. These all died in faith, not having received the things promised, but having seen them and greeted them from afar, and having acknowledged that they were strangers and exiles on the earth. (Hebrews 11:12-13)*

This is fabulous news for your home team. God has not called for perfection in your marriage. You will have seasons when you are stricken with fear of the unknown. I can only assure you that God can keep your family when you have no idea how to do so. The best thing that you can ever do for your home team is to put all of your trust and faith in Him. Faith in God was the most important thing for Abraham and Sarah. It will also be the key to their family becoming a winning home team.

What is your current position? Have you created your own tactics and have seen no progress? Well, maybe now is your breaking point. Perhaps now it is time for your breakthrough. If you have not entered a covenant relationship with Jesus, it is THE answer that you need. Your marital relationship will never get better until you have a relationship with the Creator. Let the Lord have your life and you shall be blessed. Your marriage will be blessed as result. Please do not delay!

However, maybe you are already part of the heavenly family, but you have been living according to the world's design. Maybe you have failed to allow the Word to be applied to your life or your marriage. Do you struggle to hear His voice and are not sure what to do? I want to encourage you to forsake your worldly idols and pursue the Lord. I can't tell you what He will do specifically but you should expect transformation. The Lord specializes in fixing things and people that are broken! He is just waiting for you to give Him the opportunity. Here are some things that you can apply now to get back on the right path:

- Commit to a discipleship relationship with an elder bro or sister
- Commit to your local church and submit to the leadership there
- Seek biblical counseling if needed
- Date your spouse and serve your spouse well
- Do not delay. You have nothing to lose but everything to gain

Do you need H.E.L.P.................?

H – Humble yourself and stop trying to "figure it out" on your own
E – Eliminate worldliness
L – Learn by listening more to wisdom and talking less
P – Pray for strength and guidance

Take a moment to reflect on how you can respond in the PRESENT in order to change your FUTURE.

_____

_____

_____

_____

Scriptural Index

Amos 3:3	2
Matthew 9:9	1
Matthew 11:28-30	3
Matthew 12:34b	6
Matthew 16:24	6
Matthew 18:3	1
Matthew 18:21-35	5
Matthew 18:22	5
Matthew 19:5	2
Matthew 19:8	5
Matthew 20:26	1
Mark 10:8-9	2
Mark 10:42-45	1
Luke 9:23	1
Luke 17:5	7
Luke 20:35-36	1
John 2:5	4
John 10:10	7
John 14:1-6	1
Romans 5:6-8	6
1 Corinthians 11:3	1
1 Corinthians 14:33	2
1 Corinthians 15:1	6
1 Corinthians 15:57	3
1 Corinthians 15:58	7
Galatians 6:10	2
Ephesians 4:32	2;5
Ephesians 5:22-24	1
Ephesians 5:25-26	7
Ephesians 5:31	2
Ephesians 5:34	1
1 Timothy 5:8	1
2 Timothy 1:7	1
Titus 2:4-5	1
Philippians 4:6-7	4
Hebrews 11:6	4
Hebrews 11:8	8

Bibliography

Adams, Jay. *Solving Marital Problems.* Grand Rapids: Zondervan, 1983.

Deane, William. *Abraham: His Life and Times.* London: James Nisbet and Co, 1889.

Dugid, Iain M. *Living in the Gap Between Promise and Reality.* Phillipsburg: P & R, 1999.

Eggerichs, Emerson. *Love & Respect.* Brentwood: Integrity, 2004.

Estep, Jim, Roadcup, David and Johnson, Gary. *Resolution.* Indianapolis: e2 Ministries, 2015.

Fretheim, Terrence. *Abraham: Trials of Family and Faith.* Columbia: University of South Carolina, 2007.

Gaubert, Henri. *Abraham, Loved by God.* London: Darton, Longman & Todd, 1968.

Getz, Gene. *Abraham: Holding Fast to the Will of God.* Nashville: Broadman & Holman, 1996.

Grudem, Wayne & Rainey, Dennis. *Pastoral Leadership for Manhood and Womanhood.* Wheaton: Crossway, 2002.

Hughes, Kent & Barbara. *Disciplines of a Godly Family.* Wheaton: Crossway, 1995.

Irwin, Tim. *Extraordinary Influence.* Hoboken: John Wiley & Sons, Inc., 2018.

Kostenberger, Andreas J. *God, Marriage, and Family.* Wheaton: Crossway, 2004

Maxwell, John C. *The 17 Indisputable Laws of Teamwork.* Nashville: Thomas Nelson, Inc., 2001.

Mitchell, Curtis. *God in the Garden.* New York: Doubleday & Company, 1957.

Richardson, Willie. *Reclaiming the Urban Family.* Grand Rapids: Zondervan, 1996.

Sande, Ken. *The Peacemaker.* Grand Rapids: Baker Publishing Group, 1991.

Share Your Testimony With Us

We pray that your marriage will make a kingdom sized impact on your family for generations to come. Please give us the honor of hearing how your home team has been blessed by applying the biblical principles within this book.

Email the Home Team at
info@theteamathome.com

Follow us on Social Media
Facebook: The Home Team
Instagram: @theteamathome
Twitter: @Theteamathome

Made in the
USA
Lexington, KY